.352 (41081) Wor.

The New Scottish Local Authorities

Organisation and Management Structures

Report of a working group appointed by the Scottish local authority associations:

Association of County Councils in Scotland
Convention of Royal Burghs
District Councils' Association for Scotland
Scottish Counties of Cities Association

and supported by the Secretary of State for Scotland

Presented to the Secretary of State for Scotland and the Associations, September 1973

Edinburgh   Her Majesty's Stationery Office   1973

© *Crown Copyright 1973*

Published for

Published for:
THE SCOTTISH DEVELOPMENT DEPARTMENT

ISBN 0 11 491043 X

The Working Group on Scottish Local Government Management Structures

Steering Committee

Chairman:	J. F. NIVEN, CBE	(Wigtown)
Association of County Councils in Scotland:	MAJOR A. J. MACDONALD P. M. ROBERTSON G. SHARP, OBE	(Inverness) (Ayr) (Fife)
Convention of Royal Burghs:	PROVOST J. CRAWFORD LORD PROVOST A. U. CROSS, TD EX-PROVOST E. J. DOWDALLS BAILIE J. FORDE, MBE EX-PROVOST A. C. SMYTH, OBE	(Dunfermline)[1] (Perth)[1] (Coatbridge) (Stevenston) (Forfar)
District Councils' Association for Scotland:	A. DEVLIN D. M. McBAIN	(Glenrothes) (Lairg)
Scottish Counties of Cities Association:	COUNCILLOR G. FOULKES TREASURER W. S. GRAY TREASURER MRS E. McCULLOCH COUNCILLOR R. A. RAFFAN COUNCILLOR J. SLACK TREASURER R. M. TOSH	(Edinburgh)[2] (Glasgow)[3] (Glasgow)[3] (Aberdeen) (Edinburgh)[2] (Dundee)

[1] Provost Crawford resigned in June 1972 and was replaced by Lord Provost Cross.

[2] Councillor Slack resigned in May 1973 and was replaced by Councillor Foulkes.

[3] Treasurer Gray resigned in August 1972 on his appointment as Lord Provost and was replaced by Treasurer Mrs McCulloch.

Advisory Group

Chairman:	I. V. PATERSON, CBE	(County Clerk, Lanark)
Vice-Chairman:	R. G. E. PEGGIE	(Depute City Chamberlain, Edinburgh)
Association of County Councils in Scotland:	E. GEDDES	(County Treasurer, Midlothian)
	F. INGLIS, CBE	(Secretary and Treasurer, Association of County Councils in Scotland)[1]
	G. H. SPEIRS	(Secretary and Treasurer, Association of County Councils in Scotland)[1]
Convention of Royal Burghs:	J. R. HILL	(Town Clerk, Inverness)
	J. GIBSON KERR, CBE	(Agent and Clerk, Convention of Royal Burghs)
	R. KYLE, MBE	(Town Clerk and Manager, Cumbernauld)
	A. McINTOSH	(Town Clerk, Motherwell and Wishaw)
District Councils' Association for Scotland:	J. S. CAMPBELL, MBE	(Hon. Secretary, District Councils' Association for Scotland)
	G. S. THOMSON	(Clerk, First District Council, Renfrew)
Scottish Counties of Cities Association:	DR L. BOYLE	(City Chamberlain, Glasgow)
	S. F. HAMILTON	(Depute Town Clerk, Glasgow)
Scottish Development Department:	R. D. M. BELL, CB	(Under Secretary)

[1] Mr Inglis retired in February 1973 and was replaced by Mr Speirs

iv

Central Advisory Unit

Director	G. McGowan	(P.A. Management Consultants Ltd.)
	J. H. Haddow	(Edinburgh Corporation)
	J. Maitland-Ward	(Lanark County Council)
	C. Bookless	(Midlothian County Council)

Foreword

by the Secretary of State for Scotland,
The Rt Hon Gordon Campbell, MC, MP

I am sure that everyone connected with local government in Scotland will welcome, as I do, this important report. We do not reform local government very often—the present system has hardly altered at all since 1929, and even then the changes were not as great as those which we are now undertaking. It is vital therefore that the new authorities should decide on their management structure with the best available advice before them. The management processes adopted in 1975 may have to last for many years.

All who read the report will share my appreciation of the foresight of the present local authority associations who commissioned the study for the benefit of their successors. The Government were glad to support their action and value highly the work which has been done by the Steering Committee of local authority members, the Advisory Group of officials and by the Central Advisory Unit. There is much to study in the report and all too little time for the management decisions which must be taken before May 1975.

I commend the report to all present councillors, particularly to those who will be members of the statutory advisory committees, and to prospective candidates at the 1974 elections. The report will, I hope, be the first paper to be put before those who are elected to the regional, islands and district councils.

Contents

		paragraphs	pages
Background			**xiii**
Chapter 1	**Conduct of the study**		
	Basic considerations	1.1 –1.6	1
	Conduct of the study	1.7 –1.12	2
	Order of the report	1.13	3
Chapter 2	**The basis of the proposed reform**		
	Objectives of the reform	2.1	5
	The new authorities	2.2 –2.7	6
	Constraints	2.8 –2.14	7
Chapter 3	**The current situation in Scotland**		
	The basic pattern	3.1 –3.9	9
	Recent changes	3.10–3.17	11
	Conclusions	3.18–3.20	14
Chapter 4	**Cornerstones of the new structures**		
	The fundamental need	4.1 –4.4	16
	The key roles	4.5 –4.11	17
	The corporate structure in outline	4.12–4.17	18
	The policy and resources committee	4.18–4.28	20
	The chief executive and the management team	4.29–4.35	23
Chapter 5	**The corporate management process**		
	Introduction	5.1 –5.2	26
	The process in outline	5.3 –5.6	26
	The different forms of 'planning'	5.7 –5.13	28
	A possible approach	5.14–5.16	30
	Organisational implications	5.17–5.25	32

		paragraphs	*pages*
Chapter 6	**The service functions**		
	Introduction	6.1 –6.6	**35**
	The personal services—education, social work and housing	6.7 –6.19	**36**
	Engineering and technical services	6.20–6.37	**40**
	Physical planning	6.38–6.44	**45**
	Leisure and recreation	6.45–6.54	**47**
	Consumer protection	6.55–6.58	**50**
	Environmental health	6.59–6.62	**51**
	Building control	6.63–6.67	**52**
	Police and fire services	6.68–6.71	**53**
	The assessor	6.72–6.73	**53**
	Common features of the services	6.74–6.78	**54**
Chapter 7	**The central support functions**		
	Introduction	7.1 –7.2	**55**
	Finance	7.3 –7.7	**55**
	Personnel	7.8 –7.13	**56**
	Management services	7.14–7.20	**58**
	Computer services	7.21–7.22	**60**
	Architectural services	7.23–7.31	**60**
	Legal and administrative services	7.32–7.33	**62**
	Services to members	7.34	**62**
	Estates	7.35–7.37	**63**
	Public relations	7.38–7.40	**64**
	Supplies	7.41–7.44	**64**
	Internal transport	7.45–7.46	**65**
	Property maintenance	7.47–7.49	**66**
	Common office services	7.50	**67**
	General features	7.51–7.52	**67**
Chapter 8	**Recommended structures for the new authorities**		
	The basic structure	8.1 –8.3	**68**
	The executive office	8.4 –8.9	**68**
	Regions: service committee structure	8.10–8.14	**72**
	resource committee structure	8.15–8.17	**74**
	other committees	8.18–8.20	**74**
	officer structure	8.21–8.28	**75**

			paragraphs	*pages*
Districts:	service committee			
		structure	8.29–8.32	**82**
	resource committee			
		structure	8.33–8.37	**83**
	other committees		8.38–8.39	**84**
	officer structure		8.40–8.47	**84**
Islands:	committee structure		8.48–8.57	**91**
	officer structure		8.54–8.57	**92**

Chapter 9   **Main points of the report**   9.1 –9.43   **96**

Appendices

1   Conduct of the study   **103**

2   Authorities submitting information on present organisation   **105**

3   Professional organisations submitting evidence or otherwise assisting   **107**

4   Other organisations providing assistance   **109**

5   Joint advisory committees and existing authorities submitting views on consultation paper   **111**

6   The new authorities—selected statistics   **113**

7   The proposed allocation of functions   **116**

8   Illustration of range of population of the new authorities   **118**

9   City of Dundee—new officer structure   **119**

10   Terms of reference for the policy and resources committee   **120**

11   Terms of reference for the chief executive   **121**

12   The service functions—illustrations of possible division of tasks between region and sub-region   **122**

Background

The impending reform of local government is based on the report of the Royal Commission on Local Government in Scotland (1966–1969), the Wheatley Report (Cmnd 4190), which recommended a two-tier structure of regional and district authorities. The Government's White Paper of February 1971 (Cmnd 4583) accepted the main principles stated by the Royal Commission subject to certain modifications. The Local Government (Scotland) Bill now before Parliament gives effect, with some further modifications, to the proposals outlined in the White Paper. The new councils will be elected in May 1974 and will take over in May 1975.

The White Paper (para. 75) endorsed the Commission's view that good management was vital to the effective operation of local authorities. The Government accepted that questions of internal organisation were mainly matters for each authority to decide but recognised that local authorities would wish to make a further study of these matters and the principles of management involved.

At a meeting in March 1971 between the Secretary of State for Scotland and representatives of the four Scottish local authority associations it was agreed that it would be desirable to study the organisational problems and to provide guidance on organisation and management structures for consideration by the new authorities.

The local authority associations approved a recommendation to this effect and appointed a Steering Committee of elected members from the associations to be responsible for the overall direction of the study.

The detailed direction and supervision of the study was allocated to a group of senior officials representing the four associations and the Scottish Development Department. This group, later called the Advisory Group, reached the early conclusion that, bearing in mind the extensive scope of the required investigations and the time scale within which they must be completed, there was a need for assistance from suitably qualified and experienced staff on a full-time basis. It was therefore agreed to set up a Central Advisory Unit comprising a senior management consultant and three local government officials, all on full-time secondment. The Unit became operational in June 1972.

The terms of reference agreed by the Steering Committee were to:

△ set out the considerations which should be borne in mind by local authorities in determining their structures of management at elected member and officer levels including internal arrangements bearing on efficiency in the employment of manpower;

△ advise on the formulation of patterns of organisation most likely to be suitable for the various types of authority to be established in 1974/75;

△ establish and maintain an effective liaison with local authority consultative groups, professional and staff associations, central government departments, LAMSAC, the universities and others offering a contribution to the management problems posed by reorganisation in Scotland.

The report which follows is published at the stage when the Local Government (Scotland) Bill has had its third reading in the House of Commons but is still under consideration by the House of Lords.

Chapter 1

Conduct of the Study

Basic considerations

1.1 At the outset we consider it important to set down the main factors which influenced our approach to the task. Of these, the most important is that local government exists to serve people. Although it is right that local authorities should actively pursue measures to increase their efficiency and to enhance the value obtained for ratepayers' money, such measures must not result in impairment of service to the public and lack of concern for the individual. Therefore, while we had to consider possible structures in the light of their potential effectiveness to the community as a whole, we had to avoid as far as possible the creation of large bureaucratic machines—a worry expressed by many whom we consulted.

1.2 Closely allied to this is the need to remember that local government is controlled by democratically elected members exercising powers on behalf of the community which they serve. It is fundamental therefore that decisions on policies and other major issues are the exclusive right of elected members, although officers must do much more than merely implement.

1.3 We are committed to the view that management structures are a means, not an end; they exist only to facilitate the effective performance of tasks. Therefore before considering structures in detail we paid close attention to the objectives of the services to be provided by the new authorities and to the processes needed to achieve them.

1.4 Much has already been written on the subject of management in local government by bodies such as the Maud and Mallaby Committees and the Working Party on the Staffing of Local Government in Scotland, by individuals within local government, management consultants, and by academics. In addition the results of the deliberations of our counterpart, the English Working Group on Local Authority Management Structures (the Bains Committee), were published shortly after we set about our task. We took account of all this work in our consideration of suitable structures for the new Scottish authorities.

1.5 Unlike some critics, we are not by any means convinced that all existing practices in Scottish local government are wrong. The achievements of many authorities belie this. While substantial change in some ways is certainly necessary, existing strengths must be preserved and built upon.

1.6 There exists throughout the country an immense body of experience and knowledge in the possession of elected members, officers and others who have been closely associated with local government. We drew extensively on this and wish to record our thanks and acknowledge our indebtedness to all who assisted us directly or indirectly.

Conduct of the study

1.7 It was essential that the joint committees in the areas of the new authorities should have sufficient time to consider our recommendations before preparing their own detailed proposals for the guidance of the new councils to be elected in May 1974. We therefore decided that our report had to be published by early autumn 1973 which gave us just over 12 months in which to complete our task.

1.8 In Appendix 1 we set out the main steps of the study and in Appendices 2 to 5 we list the many authorities, committees and professional and other organisations who made submissions or otherwise assisted us in our investigations.

1.9 We placed great emphasis on the need to consult widely. While it was relatively easy to do so in the case of local government officials, through their various associations, similar channels of communication with elected members were not so readily available. It was nevertheless imperative that we obtained members' views on as wide a scale as was practicable. We therefore prepared a consultation paper which attempted to summarise the basic principles which lay behind various proposed new patterns of local government organisation and which contrasted the traditional, or specialist, approach with the so-called corporate approach to management. We sent the paper to all regional, island and district joint advisory committees, inviting the views of their members on the main topics covered. The paper was given still wider circulation thereafter by some authorities, being distributed to all elected members whether or not they were members of the joint advisory committee. In all, we estimate that the document was read and considered by at least 1,000 elected members throughout Scotland.

1.10 Members' reactions were obtained either in the form of written summaries of the collective views of the committee or through replies from individual members or, in a number of cases, by attending committee meetings at which our paper was discussed.

1.11 These consultations were further supplemented by a series of visits which we made to a selected number of existing authorities of different types and sizes throughout Scotland. During these visits we met groups of members (and in one case officers) for informal discussions on the basic concepts which we had then under consideration and on their practical applicability to the new authorities.

1.12 The joint advisory committees and existing authorities from whom we obtained views are listed in Appendix 5 which also indicates those which we visited. These consultations were stimulating and invaluable and we were encouraged by the wide measure of agreement which the basic principles received and by the readiness to accept the need for change.

Order of the report

1.13 The report is set out in the following order:

△ Chapter 2 restates briefly the objectives of the reform of local government in Scotland as laid down by Wheatley and endorsed by the Government; looks at the different types and sizes of the proposed new authorities and at the functions they will perform; and instances certain constraints which will exist

△ Chapter 3 outlines the present forms of organisation found in existing Scottish authorities; looks at examples of organisational changes made in recent years; and draws some conclusions therefrom

△ Chapter 4 sets out the fundamental principles of organisation which we consider should be adopted, with only minor local variations, by the new Scottish authorities

△ Chapter 5 looks further at these fundamental principles and outlines how they might be applied in practice in terms of the processes needed to sustain them

△ Chapters 6 and 7 review the organisational characteristics and requirements of the main local government services and central support functions

△ Chapter 8 draws together the conclusions already reached and makes specific recommendations on forms of organisational structure for the different types and sizes of new authority.

Finally, in Chapter 9, we summarise the main points made throughout the report.

Chapter 2

The basis of the proposed reform

Objectives of the reform

2.1 The Wheatley Commission stated that the basic objectives of reform should be 'to secure for local government the following advantages:

Power
Local government should be enabled to play a more important, responsible and positive part in the running of the country—to bring the reality of government nearer to the people.

Effectiveness
Local government should be equipped to provide services in the most satisfactory manner, particularly from the point of view of the people receiving the services.

Local Democracy
Local government should constitute a system in which power is exercised through the elected representatives of the people, and in which those representatives are locally accountable for its exercise.

Local Involvement
Local government should bring the people into the process of reaching decisions as much as possible, and enable those decisions to be made intelligible to the people.'

The Government in its White Paper endorsed these objectives and expressed its belief that 'these are the cornerstones on which the new structure must be founded'. These objectives will require to be achieved within the framework laid down for the new authorities in the Local Government (Scotland) Bill now before Parliament.

The new authorities

2.2 The Bill provides for a two-level structure of regions and districts throughout Scotland except for Orkney, Shetland and the Western Isles, which will be islands areas and will be most-purpose authorities. Appendix 6 sets out certain statistics in respect of each of the new authorities, and Appendix 7 lists the allocation of functions.

2.3 There are substantial variations in population and geographical area as between the new authorities. In Appendix 8 we show diagrammatically the wide range of population differences. Some interesting comparisons emerge; for example,

△ Strathclyde Region contains almost as many people as all other regions put together

△ Glasgow City District is larger in population than any of the regions except Strathclyde

△ just over one third (17) of the proposed districts are larger in population than the Borders region

△ four districts each have a population smaller than the average population of one ward in Glasgow City District

2.4 Similarly, in geographical area,

△ Highland Region is more extensive than the next two largest regions (Strathclyde and Grampian) combined

△ four districts (Argyll, Perth and Kinross, Skye and Lochalsh, Ross and Cromarty) each cover a wider area than four of the regions (Borders, Central, Fife, Lothian).

2.5 In terms of functions, the standard allocation as between regions and districts is departed from within the Highland, Borders, and Dumfries and Galloway Regions. In these three areas the Government have taken the view that the districts will not have the resources needed to provide a satisfactory service in the fields of local planning and of libraries. These functions are to be undertaken by the region. Building control, which has close affinities with local planning, will also be exercised by the region.

6

2.6 The regional and district areas are so diverse in population, area and in other characteristics that it is obvious there is no single structure which could be universally suitable to every authority of the same type. While the basic organisational principles set out in Chapter 4 are applicable to all of the new authorities, the extent to which they are applied, and the staff and the degree of sophistication of the processes needed to sustain them, will vary substantially across the country.

2.7 We have tried to indicate throughout the report the ways in which we feel our main conclusions could be modified to take account of these differences, but have not attempted to provide answers to detailed questions peculiar to individual areas. These we feel will be best resolved by the members and officers with specific local knowledge and experience.

Constraints

2.8 Our remit has been to produce recommendations on organisation and management structures to fit the new form of local government as specified in the Local Government (Scotland) Bill, not to comment on the Bill itself. However, certain features of the proposed reform impose some constraints on the choice of types of structure for the new authorities.

2.9 In all but three of the regions the planning function is split, major planning and related services being allocated to the region and local planning and associated services to the district. In addition, certain functions with strong interdependencies, such as social work and housing, have been made the responsibility of different levels while other functions, such as recreation, are to be exercised concurrently by both levels. Later in our report we endorse the need for the corporate approach within local government and seek to establish the unified nature of the overall planning process. The proposed allocation of functions militates somewhat against achievement of the desired unity and precludes certain organisational possibilities which might otherwise have been desirable.

2.10 The Bill makes mandatory the establishment of education and social work committees and the appointment of certain officers, including directors of education and of social work. Again, these provisions restrict the possible committee and officer arrangements.

7

2.11 Other constraints are imposed by the necessity to appoint joint committees for police and fire in certain areas and by the requirement to set up school and college councils.

2.12 The wide divergencies in size as between authorities have already been instanced. In the unique case of Strathclyde, the conflict between the objectives of local democracy and involvement on the one hand and of effective policy direction and control on the other is likely to be most acute. This is acknowledged in the Bill by the requirement for the Strathclyde Regional Council to submit, for the Secretary of State's approval, their proposed arrangements for the discharge of their education and social work functions.

2.13 Summing up, therefore, the reform is founded on laudable objectives but the practical achievement of these objectives will depend to an extent on overcoming the constraints imposed by certain of the statutory provisions.

2.14 We now review the current situation in Scotland to see what lessons are offered.

Chapter 3

The current situation in Scotland

The basic pattern

3.1 With certain significant exceptions, which we examine in the next section of this chapter, the structure found in most Scottish authorities is still largely traditional. Historically, as obligations have been placed on local authorities to provide particular services, new committees and departments have been grafted on to the existing structure. As a result, a high degree of specialisation or departmentalism is found. This was reflected in the information supplied to us by most of the authorities listed at Appendix 2.

3.2 The number of standing committees in the four cities ranged from 13 to 22. The number most frequently found in counties and also in large burghs was 10, with a range from 7 to 15, although one county in fact has 25 standing committees. In the small burghs the most frequent number was 6, with a range from 4 to 15.

3.3 In all types of authority the most usual size of committee was between 30 per cent and 40 per cent of the full council membership. Conveners' and provosts' committees, because of their particular functions, tended to have a lower membership, usually between 10 per cent and 20 per cent of the full council. On the other hand four large burghs indicated that all or most of their committees consisted of the full, or almost the full, council. Nine small burghs which replied also said that they followed this practice although all had a total council membership of 12 or fewer.

3.4 Notwithstanding the co-ordinating role performed by clerks and chief financial officers, the general picture of the structure at officer level is that of a number of independent departments whose heads are directly responsible to a committee or group of committees. Within counties and large burghs the usual number of departments is around 14 or 15, and in the cities from 22 to over 30. At the other end of the scale, most small burghs, with their limited range of functions, have between 2 and 4 departments.

3.5 In general, the process of formulating policies and devising plans to implement these policies is carried out independently within the various service committees and their respective departments, each making separate recommendations to the full council. Although there is now widespread recognition that the activities of any one committee or department interact to a substantial degree with those of other parts of the organisation, particularly in terms of their end-effect on the public, there is still very little in the way of formal co-ordination across the whole range of an authority's activities.

3.6 At committee level, such co-ordination as does exist usually takes place in the finance committee which, in the absence of any other committee charged with co-ordination of policy, attempts to fill the gap. However, while the finance committee does exert some overall influence, the effectiveness of this is limited because:

△ its members are in no position to assess whether the sum total of the various departmental spending proposals really represents a cohesive programme geared to achieve the authority's objectives (which in most cases have never been defined specifically)

△ they lack guidelines to assist them in reconciling the competing claims of the various services for finance

△ they are concerned only with the financial implications of the departmental programmes and not with the deployment of other important elements of resource necessary for the implementation of the programmes.

In addition the finance committee's involvement usually occurs only after the spending committees' plans are at an advanced stage, when it is much more difficult to bring about major changes.

3.7 It was suggested to us in some authorities that across-the-board co-ordination is effectively achieved through the convener's or provost's committee. Our investigations lead us to believe however that the terms of reference of these committees are limited in most cases to considering only those matters which do not fall within the remit of other committees, to arbitration between committees in cases of dispute or to handling emergency situations. Even in the few cases where their terms of reference go beyond this and include some co-ordinating role, again the major drawback appears to be that any co-ordination which takes place is usually 'after the event'—at the stage, in other words, when individual committees' planning is at a very advanced stage and therefore not at all easy to influence or alter in a major way.

3.8 The extent to which responsibility is devolved from the full council to its committees and to officers varies extensively from authority to authority and no one typical pattern emerges clearly. In general, we found a greater unwillingness to delegate among smaller authorities. In the larger authorities the sheer volume of work necessitates some delegation if the despatch of business is not to be seriously impeded.

3.9 In many authorities, particularly in the more industrialised and urban areas, organised political groups have a significant influence on the decision-making process While decisions are still taken formally within the authority's committees, the decision-making process in relation to major and politically sensitive issues takes place outwith the council chamber at meetings of the majority party group and its executive. Like Wheatley, we have found no real evidence that the group system militates against effectiveness. On the contrary, it has been suggested to us that the existence of a strong group produces benefits in terms of coherence and consistency of approach. We return later to consideration of the group system and its relationships with the formal committee structure and with officers. At this point we would merely endorse the Wheatley Commission's opinion: 'Whatever view may be taken on this issue, party politics must be accepted as a fact of life. They can neither be legislated for, nor legislated out of existence; and it is a mistake to allow feelings on the matter to influence the choice of a management structure.'

Recent changes

3.10 Of the authorities who provided us with information on their existing structures just over 20 per cent reported having made significant changes in organisation in recent years, following the publication of the Maud and Mallaby Reports. A few others have contemplated major revisions but eventually decided against implementation, mainly because of the impending reorganisation of local government.

3.11 The most usual change reported was a reduction in the number of committees, sometimes accompanied by an increase in committee membership. In most cases the extent of the reduction was small, although several burghs did in fact halve their numbers. There is some encouraging evidence of a trend towards the grouping of related activities within the remits to committees. Several authorities for example have appointed a civic amenities committee which is concerned broadly with provision for leisure and has responsibility within its overall remit for the parks, baths and museums departments and, in some cases, libraries. These services were previously the responsibility of separate committees.

3.12 Some authorities have formalised their policy-making arrangements by appointing policy committees and others are presently considering a similar step. This innovation is aimed at meeting the need for a body at elected member level able to take an overview of the authority's activities across departmental boundaries, to assess priorities and to consider the allocation of resources. We take four authorities—Glasgow, Greenock, Coatbridge and East Kilbride—as examples to illustrate the composition and terms of reference of these new committees.

3.13 The present composition of the four policy committees (in Greenock called the policy and resources committee) is as follows:

Glasgow   12 members, all from the majority party (total council 111)

Greenock   6 members, 5 from the majority party (total council 27)

Coatbridge   16 members, 14 from the majority party (total council 18)

East Kilbride   10 members, all from the majority party (total council 18).

3.14 There are certain differences in the terms of reference given to the committees, as will be seen from the wording of the following extracts:

Glasgow 'while having no executive powers . . . reviewing from time to time the general economic and financial policy of the Corporation, including the allocation of resources in terms of manpower and finance'

Greenock 'to guide the council in the formulation of its corporate plan of objectives and priorities, and for this purpose to recommend to the council such forward programmes and other steps as may be necessary to achieve those objectives either in whole or in part, during specific time spans'

'without prejudice to the duties and responsibilities of the service committees, to review the effectiveness of all the council's work and the standards and levels of service provided. To identify the need for new services and to keep under review the necessity for existing ones'

Coatbridge 'determining the council's overall objectives'

'consideration and review of the objectives and action plans for each of the council's services and, on the basis of this review, allocation of resources between committees and deciding priorities'

East Kilbride 'to consider and review from time to time the policies and priorities of the town council both generally and in relation to specific functions and projects and to report thereon to the council with recommendations'

It will be seen from the foregoing that the initial remit in Glasgow has been somewhat more cautious, and in Coatbridge rather more radical, than the other two authorities.

3.15 On the officer side, we know of at least nine authorities which have re-designated their clerk as clerk and chief executive or equivalent title, formally recognised as head of the team of chief officers and with duties and responsibilities defined along the lines proposed by Maud and by the Working Party on the Staffing of Local Government in Scotland. Four of these authorities have also concluded that their chief executive should be freed from direct line management of a major department, in order to enable him to devote maximum attention to across-the-board co-ordination and control, and have set up separate legal departments under officials of chief officer status.

3.16 Apart from the necessary changes resulting from the Social Work (Scotland) Act 1968, we have found little evidence of widespread reorganisation of departmental structures and groupings. Two large burgh authorities have set up technical services departments embracing the functions of engineering, master of works, architecture, surveying, planning, property maintenance and, in one case, parks and amenities.

3.17 Dundee has recently approved a major restructuring of departments and is now in the course of implementing the necessary changes. The new departmental structure is illustrated at Appendix 9. It embodies certain important concepts, particularly that of the 'executive office', which we examine in Chapter 8.

Conclusions

3.18 Our review of the existing scene has confirmed our previous belief that most Scottish local authorities are still organised on the traditional departmental basis. It has also shown, however, that some councils have become increasingly aware of the limitations which the traditional set-up imposes on the development of comprehensive policies and cohesive programmes of action properly geared to meet the needs of the community. While only a small number of authorities have as yet taken positive measures to rectify the situation, we perceive a real acceptance among members and officials of the need for change, particularly in the light of the proposals for reform.

3.19 We believe that the traditional type of organisation does possess certain strengths, not least of which is its professionalism. The specialist approach to particular aspects of local government services has resulted in expert knowledge backed by a wealth of experience on the part of both elected members and officers always being available to meet the growing complexity of today's activities. However this very professionalism has helped to foster the excessive departmentalism which is perhaps the main weakness in the existing management of local government in Scotland. The words of Maud are equally applicable to Scotland: 'there may be unity in the parts but there is disunity in the whole . . . Planning for the development of the community, the allocation of priorities for finance or for space on the drawing board, the timing of various schemes, all demand a co-ordinated approach.'

3.20 What is required for the new authorities is a form of organisation which will at the same time:

△ provide the means of achieving a unified approach to the formulation and implementation of policies and plans to meet the real needs of the community,

△ preserve the strengths of the expert professional approach which will still be required for the effective discharge of the local authority's functions,

△ ensure a challenging and worthwhile role for elected members and officers, and

△ be sufficiently flexible to adapt and respond quickly to change.

We now proceed to consider how these objectives might be achieved.

Chapter 4

Cornerstones of
the new structures

The fundamental need

4.1 In this chapter we set out certain fundamental principles which must, in our view, be basic elements in the structures of all of the new authorities however much these may vary in detail. In doing so we re-state and endorse much which has already been said by others such as Maud, Wheatley and Bains. The pedigree of the basic concepts is irreproachable and the message is vital enough to bear —and indeed to demand—repetition.

4.2 The Royal Commission on Local Government in England defined the substance of local government as 'an all round responsibility for the safety, health and wellbeing, both material and cultural, of people in different localities in so far as these objectives can be achieved by local action and local initiative within a framework of national policy'. In fact and in law, local authorities have never enjoyed power commensurate with such an all-round responsibility. Local authorities have not had, and are still not being given, a 'general competence'. Nevertheless, we would accept entirely the spirit behind the definition. Within the bounds of law and the limitations imposed by the proposed form and functions of the new authorities we have no doubt that the new authorities must be wide-ranging in their consideration of community needs and must look beyond the immediate confines of an individual service or a single year's estimates.

4.3 During our investigations we have had many examples quoted to us of the serious adverse effects resulting from insufficient co-ordination—housing developments lacking in community facilities; education and housing provisions out of phase with each other; social work problems created by unilateral action taken elsewhere in the organisation; wasteful duplication of facilities—and doubtless the readers of this report could cite many more.

4.4 We regard as established beyond all question the need in principle for the corporate approach—not just within a single authority but between authorities and with central government.

The key roles

4.5 Before proceeding to consider the fundamental elements of a corporate structure, we think it necessary to state our views on the functions of the council and on the respective roles of elected members and officials.

4.6 In the words of Wheatley, 'the council should provide a forum for public debate and for the open challenge and questioning of policy and its application. It is in the council chamber that local democracy should be at its most visible'. The council is the body in which the authority's broad objectives and the major commitment of resources should be fully discussed and decided. Our own judgement and the strong opinions expressed to us by members commit us to Wheatley's view that 'no form of internal organisation can be acceptable if it treats the council as a mere talking shop, assembly or showplace, while the real business is done elsewhere'. The power of decision-making must in the end remain with the council.

4.7 To exercise this role effectively the council must receive the best possible advice on a co-ordinated basis not solely from its officers but also, in all but the smallest authorities, from an appropriate body of its own members. We shortly consider how this might be provided.

4.8 The idea that policy is a matter exclusively for elected members and administration exclusively for officers is, in our view, unrealistic although it is disturbing to find, as the Bains Report comments, that 'many members and officers still see this as a sufficient description of their respective roles and one behind which they can shelter as occasion requires'. Bains recognised that both elements were present in different degrees at every stage of the management process, the balance on the scale shifting progressively from member control with officer advice at the 'policy setting' end to officer control with member advice at the 'execution' end.

4.9 Some members have suggested to us that they are forced to become involved in details because officials are unwilling to take decisions; we accept that this is sometimes the case. On the other hand, we are aware of many instances of members regularly reserving to themselves routine, low-level decision-making which could only remotely be construed as essential to the democratic process. The principle should be that issues are dealt with at the lowest level consistent with the nature of the problem. Where this level will actually be will vary depending on the size of an authority and on other local factors.

4.10 The need for greater devolution of decision-taking is accepted by most Scottish members and officials with whom we have consulted, subject to the demands of the member's constituency role which will occasionally necessitate some involvement in matters of detailed execution.

4.11 Wheatley said that the member's role 'has two main essential elements, the managerial and the representative. The first is exercised collectively, the second on a very personal and individual basis. This is not to say that the two are wholly distinct from one another. They interact'. This view accords with our own and is akin to the earlier point made about the member/officer relationship in that separation of the member's policy-making and constituency roles is artificial. Sensitivity to and awareness of local needs and feelings are fundamental to sound policy-making and to the assessment of the practical results of implementation. Recognising this, some authorities make a point of inviting participation in committee discussion by the local member when issues of particular concern to his constituency are under consideration. We think this practice should be more widely adopted.

The corporate structure in outline

4.12 We have referred above (para. 4.7) to the need in all but the smallest authorities for a body of members responsible for the preparation of advice to the council on major policy, priorities and allocation of financial, manpower and land resources; within this task we would also include reviewing the effectiveness of the action taken to implement the policy decided upon by the council. Our consultations revealed that the vast majority of members and officers in Scottish local government agree with this basic need.

4.13 Although many different forms have been suggested for this central co-ordinating body, essentially they fall into three basic types:

cabinet

management board

policy committee.

Wheatley, while not passing final judgement, outlined the main features of each type, and set down clearly their respective advantages and disadvantages, in Appendix 25 to his report.

4.14 In the cabinet system there would be a leader and several 'ministers' each directly responsible for a particular service; any committees other than the cabinet itself would be advisory only; chief officers would be answerable to their ministers and subject to only general co-ordination by the chief executive officer. In the management board system committees would be deliberative and representative, not executive; chief officers would take instructions from the council and the management board through the chief executive officer.

4.15 Among the advantages claimed for the cabinet and management board systems are that they would:

△ provide for the quick and efficient despatch of business, and

△ provide a clear avenue of approach and answerability by chief officers.

A few individual councillors and a small number of officers' professional associations have indicated that they favour one or other of these approaches for the new Scottish authorities.

4.16 In our view, however, these claimed advantages are outweighed by the restrictions which such systems would place on participation by all members in the affairs of the authority. The management board system as advocated by Maud implies that other committees of the authority would have no directing or controlling role but would be only deliberative bodies; under the cabinet system it is doubtful whether there is any place for committees at all, even in an advisory capacity. It is significant that of all the structural changes made by authorities, both English and Scottish, since the publication of the Maud Report not one to the best of our knowledge is based on the cabinet or management board systems. We reject any form of organisation based on either of these systems.

4.17 It seems to us that the best balance between the conflicting demands of effectiveness and democracy is struck by the policy committee type of approach. Because it is, in our view, impracticable to consider policy in the abstract without reference to the resources needed for implementation, we prefer the title of policy and resources committee, as advocated by Bains and others.

The policy and resources committee

4.18 The functions of the policy and resources committee are well described in the observations made to us by the Joint Advisory Committee of the Strathclyde Region. 'The Policy and Resources Committee should have more than a co-ordinating role. It should be responsible for identifying and setting out for consideration by the whole council the fundamental objectives which the council should be aiming to achieve, charting the broad course to be followed and setting the policy guidelines. It should also be charged with responsibility for co-ordinating the activities of other committees and for recommending how disputes between such committees might be resolved. It should have a free-ranging remit enabling it to monitor and review the performance of service committees and departments towards the attainment of the Council's objectives'. This accords closely with the suggested terms of reference for the policy and resources committee which we have set out in Appendix 10.

4.19 We consider it important to underline the relationship between the policy and resources committee and the service committees. We have already indicated our belief that the strengths of the specialist approach should be preserved in whatever new forms of organisation are finally implemented by the new authorities. We think it essential therefore that, within the framework of the overall policy plan, the service committees continue to be responsible for policy formulation and implementation within their own particular spheres of interest. Again, we feel that the observations of the Strathclyde Joint Advisory Committee are pertinent, '. . . the Policy and Resources Committee should be able to review the performance of other committees as against the Council's declared aims and objectives and to submit reports on the results of the reviews to the service committees and to the council for any necessary action. It should not, however, interfere with the making of policy decisions by the programme or service committees within the ambit of the overall plan except where such decisions impinged on the interests of other committees. The programme or service committees should not be subordinate to the Policy and Resources Committee and should enjoy the same right of direct access to the Council.'

4.20 On the question of resources a distinction can be made between:

△ the major policy area concerned with overall deployment of resources in line with assessed priorities, and

△ the on-going task of detailed allocation and management of the individual resource elements of finance, manpower and land.

The former must clearly be the province of the policy and resources committee. The latter task would also be undertaken by the policy and resources committee in the smaller authorities as we suggest in Chapter 8. In larger authorities, however, the probable scale of activities could render this impracticable, and separate committees may be necessary. Where this is the case, strong links between these and the policy and resources committee are, in our view, essential. The resource committees could either be regarded as linked or supportive committees to the policy and resources committee, with a substantial amount of common membership, or could be sub-committees of the policy and resources committee as proposed by Bains. Local circumstances will dictate which alternative is preferable.

4.21 The monitoring and review of performance against the authority's agreed objectives is a vital task—so vital in fact that we see this as a major function of the policy and resources committee itself and as an integral part of the continuing cyclical process. Therefore we would not envisage this task being allocated to a performance review sub-committee as suggested by Bains. For the same reason we would not support the interesting suggestion made to us by several elected members, that the review function should be carried out by a separate committee consisting as they put it 'entirely of back-bench members and conducting its affairs somewhat along the lines of a Parliamentary select committee'. While we think that this type of committee could be useful in certain particular situations, we believe that it does not recognise the fundamental differences in the nature and practice of local, as opposed to central, government and that it does not give the review function its essential place as an integral and central part of the corporate structure.

4.22 While there is widespread agreement on the need for a body akin to the policy and resources committee as we have defined it, there are differences of view as to its composition. Final decisions on this matter can only be made by the members of the new authorities themselves.

4.23 In our view it is of paramount importance that the committee should be strong and influential and able to command the support of the council and the other committees. For this reason we would reject any suggestion that it should consist entirely of back-bench members. In any group of people there are always some who by virtue of their personal attributes will be the acknowledged leaders and opinion formers. In principle, therefore, the bulk of policy and resources committee membership should be drawn from their ranks. In practice, the majority are also likely to be conveners of other major committees.

4.24 We have earlier mentioned the differences in the level of organised political activity in different parts of Scotland and have recognised that the majority party group is in some cases the real decision-making body. Where this applies we believe that it should be openly acknowledged and given recognition in the authority's procedures.

4.25 Regarding the composition of the policy and resources committee, possible alternatives are:

△ to have the policy and resources committee consist solely of the majority party with suitable provision for keeping minority parties adequately informed

△ to have minority party representation on the main committee but to set up a sub-committee consisting of majority party representatives only

△ to have a multi-party committee and to set up suitable procedures for briefing the party groups.

4.26 Advocates of minority party representation have suggested that in addition to being more democratic, such representation could help to provide better continuity of the authority's affairs; a single-party system, they claim, could lead to a wholesale reversal of policies when control of the council changed hands. Our experience suggests, however, that such radical reversals across the whole field of the authority's activities are seldom feasible in practice, while policy changes in contentious areas, involving as they usually do fundamental differences in party ideologies, are to be expected as a basic result of the democratic process irrespective of the composition of a policy and resources committee or indeed of its existence.

4.27 In practice, in many authorities with highly organised political parties, the single party approach will be adopted by the majority party and accepted, and perhaps even tacitly endorsed, by the minority. Whatever approach is adopted we stress the need to make effective arrangements for the provision of officer advice to the party groups prior to decisions being taken. We believe that elected members would welcome this, and indeed we know that it already happens in some authorities, albeit unofficially. We would urge the new authorities to adopt a similarly realistic attitude.

4.28 To be properly effective we consider that the size of the policy and resources committee must be kept to reasonable proportions consistent with an adequate level of representation. Our view is that the minimum membership should be around 8 and the maximum between 12 and 15, depending on the size of the council.

The chief executive and the management team

4.29 The need for corporate arrangements at the officer level is so widely accepted that we believe we can now take as read the necessity for a cohesive team of officers with an acknowledged leader working to a common set of objectives.

4.30 In all the evidence which we received from members and officers alike there was almost unanimous support for the appointment of an officer recognised as the head of the authority's paid service, accountable to the council for the provision of co-ordinated advice and the effective implementation of agreed policies and plans, and with direct authority over and responsibility for all other officers except where they are carrying out statutory duties or are exercising their professional judgement.

4.31 A variety of terms of reference have been proposed for the chief executive as we prefer to call him; we set out our recommended version at Appendix 11. We accept that the post of chief executive should be open to anyone of the requisite calibre irrespective of professional qualifications. Personal qualities and proven leadership ability of the highest order will be necessary. The chief executive will play a key role and it is critical that authorities make the right appointment to this position.

4.32 It has been said that the chief executive should not have direct responsibility for a major department in the traditional sense of the clerk's or treasurer's department, except in the smaller authorities. We would accept this. In the larger authorities, however, we are convinced that the chief executive will need a substantial degree of support if he is to perform his task effectively. We have given careful consideration to the form this support might take and we favour the concept of the 'executive office' which we discuss in Chapter 8.

4.33 The role of the officers' management team is to act as the focal point for the preparation and presentation to the council, via the policy and resources committee and the service committees, of co-ordinated advice on policies and major programmes of work. This implies a commitment on the part of all members of the team to act with the wider objectives of the whole authority in mind, not being concerned solely with the activities and interests of their own particular departments. We consider that this is a realistic and indeed essential aim. It is consistent with good management theory and practice and we can see no reason why it should not be applicable within local government.

4.34 Evidence on the optimum size of the management team is varied. We accept the general principle that it should be kept to a small number to facilitate discussion and decision-taking. This principle, however, should be conditioned by the need to ensure adequate representation and utilisation of the different skills available within the authority and to secure the necessary degree of commitment and involvement. There is no magic number which governs the size of the team.

4.35 In this chapter we have attempted to lay the basic foundations. We would stress that the corporate approach is not merely a question of structure—equally important are the processes needed to sustain it and the genuine willingness of all concerned to make it work in practice. The former we consider in the next chapter; the latter we leave to the good sense of the members and officers who will serve the new authorities.

Chapter 5

The corporate management process

Introduction

5.1 We have chosen to call this chapter 'The Corporate Management Process' rather than 'The Corporate Planning Process' not only because of the confusion and uncertainty surrounding the meaning of the word 'planning' in local government circles—a confusion which we attempt to dispel later in this chapter—but rather because we are considering and advocating a total style of management, not merely an isolated technique. It is vital therefore that the process of formulating objectives and programmes of action is not seen as a thing apart; it is the whole core of the authority's activity.

5.2 We do not see it as our task to provide a detailed manual of guidance because what is appropriate in one authority may well be inappropriate elsewhere unless substantially modified. We have concentrated on trying to highlight the main features of the process, in particular the practical stages which may be gone through and their organisational implications. While the principles are applicable in all authorities the scale and extent of their application must clearly be tailored to suit the needs of, and the means available to, each particular authority.

The process in outline

5.3 The ultimate objective of corporate management is to achieve a situation where the needs of a community are viewed comprehensively and the activities of the local authority are planned, directed and controlled in a unified manner to satisfy those needs to the maximum extent consistent with available resources. The main steps in the process can be summarised as follows:

△ to identify and as far as possible measure and analyse existing needs and new (and changing) problems within the community served by the authority

△ to specify the desired objectives for the provision of services to meet those needs and to quantify them

△ to consider the various alternative means of achieving these objectives

△ to evaluate the various means and in the light of the assessment of resources required and benefits expected to decide on the best means

△ in so doing to examine the inter-relationships and inter-actions of the different departments of the authority

△ to produce action programmes covering several years ahead to achieve the stated objectives

△ to implement the action programmes

△ to carry out a systematic and continuous review of the programmes in the light of progress made and of changing circumstances, and

△ to measure real achievement in relation to the stated objectives.

An essential characteristic of the process is its continuous or cyclical nature.

5.4 The concept of corporate management has occasionally been criticised as being oriented towards the needs of officers rather than of members. Properly applied, however, we feel that the reverse is in fact the case. During our visits to authorities we were often met with the complaint from members that either they were given insufficient information on alternative courses of action or else presented, as a recent statement from the Institute of Municipal Treasurers and Accountants puts it, '. . . with a mass of paper and piles of ad hoc reports often with little apparent link between them. Beyond the scope of the report immediately in front of him an elected member may well find it difficult to get a comprehensive picture of the local authority as a whole and its impact on the life of the community.'

5.5 The Institute's statement goes on to say: 'In seeking a sound management system for the authority as a whole the key really lies in establishing a framework that will link together all the various aspects at both member and officer level. Through such a medium members would be provided with the comprehensive picture referred to earlier, individual reports could be considered in perspective and decisions taken with a fuller knowledge of their implications.'

5.6 This view accords closely with our own. Furthermore, the practical experience of those authorities which have actually implemented some form of corporate management suggests that elected members have found their scope for effective decision-making and control significantly improved.

The different forms of 'planning'

5.7 Before looking at the practical steps which might be taken towards the implementation of a corporate system of management, we feel it necessary to digress somewhat in order to try to dispel certain possible misconceptions. We are aware that there are many people within local government in Scotland who perceive quite clearly and correctly the relationship between corporate management in the round and the various forms of 'planning' which already exist or have been mooted. However, there are many who do not and we consider it necessary to define what we mean.

5.8 We stressed at the beginning of this chapter that we are concerned with a total system of management—not just planning what is to be done but actually doing it, controlling how it is done, monitoring the results achieved, adapting in the light of experience and carrying out the whole process in a concerted, or corporate manner. Planning, therefore, is only a part of the total management process, albeit a most important part and perhaps the least well developed in Scottish local government today.

5.9 When referring, in the corporate sense, to the task of planning what is to be done we use the term 'policy planning', the core of which is the authority's policy plan. This should define the council's policies on those matters which are in the council's control or over which it can exert influence; the policy plan should state in broad terms how the council seeks to achieve its objectives, and its priorities for doing so, and should have regard not simply to what the council wishes to do but also to its capacity to carry out its plans. The policy plan, in other words, must be the master from which all other plans of the authority should be derived and to which they would all contribute. These other plans would include not only the plans or programmes of the various service departments, and the budgets and manpower plans, but also any others which the authority may be required to prepare, particularly those required under town and country planning legislation.

5.10 The relationship of the policy plan to the service or departmental plans and to finance and manpower budgets is reasonably clear; the policy plan sets the overall scene in terms of major policy, objectives, priorities and overall allocation of resources; the others give detailed expression to the policy plan in terms of policies and programmes for the various services and the resultant total demands of these on the authority's finance and manpower resources.

5.11 In the case of town and country planning, the relationship with the policy plan is less clear and needs further elaboration. The confusion stems initially from the identification in local government of the word 'planning' with the land use and physical planning process. The present form of development plan, although it was intended to reflect all underlying policy decisions of the authority, is still in practice confined almost solely to land use. Under the Town and Country Planning (Scotland) Act 1972, however, a new system of structure plans and local plans is prescribed. The new system is intended to embrace specifically all policies of the authority, social and economic as well as those which directly affect the physical environment, whether or not these policies are implemented under town and country planning procedures. Thus there are areas of common interest between the policy plan and structure and local plans. Structure and local plans also have an impact beyond an authority's immediate sphere of control in that they affect other authorities and also organisations outwith local government.

5.12 The similarities between policy planning and structure planning have led some people to believe that the structure plan will become, in effect, the authority's policy plan. We consider this to be a misconception because:

△ although the structure plan is concerned with economic, social and environmental ends, it is still orientated towards the specification of purely physical means

△ the statutory basis of structure planning entails a degree of rigidity which is out of keeping with the flexibility which must be inherent in policy planning.

We therefore see structure planning as only part of the total policy planning process. The structure plan can neither be isolated from, nor developed as a substitute for, the policy plan.

5.13 The formulation of policy plan and structure plan proposals is, in our view, the central task of the policy and resources committee. To attain the necessary degree of involvement and commitment, contributions to the central policy planning procedure must be drawn from virtually all parts of the authority. It follows that responsibility for co-ordinating the formulation of policy plan proposals should be attached to the chief executive and the executive office, as we describe later in Chapter 8. In Chapter 8 also, when we refer to a planning and development committee for certain authorities, we intend that its duties should be concerned only with the land use aspects of structure and local plans and, where appropriate, with development control.

A possible approach

5.14 Practical experience of policy planning in Scottish authorities is as yet meagre. We have, however, taken account of developments in English authorities and we are indebted to the staff of the Institute of Local Government Studies and to individual authorities such as the City of Coventry for the provision of much relevant and useful material.

5.15 The comprehensive approach to policy planning would involve the adoption of a total system such as Planning, Programming, Budgetting (PPBS). The so-called gradualist approach seeks to be more selective and confines itself, at least in the early stages of development, to concentrating on selected key areas.

5.16 PPBS has much to commend it, but it is sophisticated and expensive to install, particularly in the early development stages of policy planning. In its fully developed form, also, it may not be entirely appropriate in a political atmosphere. The system would also take some years to install. Therefore, in new authorities there is really no practical alternative in the initial years to the adoption of the gradualist approach, the main elements or stages in which could be as follows:

△ the production of a document or series of documents summarising the authority's existing policies and activities (sometimes called a position statement)

△ the production of a statement of the council's policies, objectives and priorities for the future; of necessity, this may be rough and ready and largely unquantified in the early stages and may require to be substantially refined as better information becomes available; ultimately, however, this document (or policy plan) and the supporting detailed departmental plans and budgets will form the kernel of the authority's corporate management system

△ the identification of areas where gaps or shortfalls from the desirable level of service are known or suspected to exist; again this may require to be done fairly intuitively in the early stages

△ from this, the selection of key areas for investigation in depth by multi-disciplinary teams; this stage is usually called policy analysis or review

△ the development of improved financial budgetting procedures, covering both capital and revenue expenditure, on a rolling programme basis for at least five years forward

△ the gradual build-up of a comprehensive management information system; this would probably be computer-based and centred on the region although not totally located there; it should draw together into a readily usable form the mass of relevant information already available not just within the region itself but within the districts and from government departments and other central sources

△ the initiation of research to fill information gaps in the selected key areas and the feeding of the research results into the management information system

△ the integration of all planning and budgetting into a unified system carried out on a cyclical basis in phase with annual estimates procedures.

Organisational implications

5.17 We have already outlined the roles of the council, the policy and resources committee, the service committees, and the chief executive and his management team in the corporate management process. Our further consideration of the process and of the possible development of a unified policy planning procedure suggests additional requirements in terms of organisation.

5.18 In principle, committees and departments of the authority should be organised as far as possible on a 'programme area' basis —that is, the grouping together, in some form, of activities which are closely related in terms of their purpose or end-result. During our consultations we have found a wide measure of agreement on this concept among elected members and officers and indeed, as we have mentioned earlier in our report, there are some indications that a few authorities have already moved in this direction.

5.19 The grouping of services into the same programme area does not of course necessitate the creation of a permanent grouping or amalgamation of departments. There is no absolute requirement for the departmental structure to mirror the programme areas if inappropriate or unwieldy groupings would result.

5.20 Where a number of departments fall within one programme area multi-disciplinary groups of officers (programme area teams) could readily be set up. Depending on the circumstances, the members of these teams might be seconded from relevant departments on a full-time or a part-time basis. This type of arrangement commends itself to us for several reasons. It encourages corporate involvement and commitment by officers at a variety of levels from a number of departments and provides them with an opportunity to gain valuable experience as members of a team. It also maintains a degree of flexibility needed in an effective corporate system.

5.21 The foregoing arrangements would provide a suitable basis for operating the corporate process in most authorities. In the larger regions, however, we consider that they would require to be reinforced in two ways because of the greater scale and complexity of operations.

5.22 First we believe that there is a need for a policy planning unit as part of the executive office. The unit's role would be to service the chief executive and his management team and the policy and resources committee by providing detailed assistance in such tasks as:

△   identification and formulation of objectives

△   evaluation of programmes

△   provision of specialist advice to programme area teams

△   monitoring and review of progress against plans

△   overall co-ordination of the policy planning process.

The unit would consist of a nucleus of permanent specialists together with a complement of staff seconded from the service departments as required.

5.23 Second there is a requirement for a central research and intelligence capability. Wheatley aptly described intelliegence as 'the handmaiden of all the functions' and we have already implied in our outline description of a possible corporate process that the availability of reliable information is fundamental to effective policy planning. We would accept that certain research may be more appropriately carried out by service departments and that they may also have certain unique information requirements. The total effort, however, must be co-ordinated centrally to ensure consistency of approach and maximum availability of information in a usable form.

5.24 Finally, we must stress the vital necessity for close and harmonious co-operation among authorities. In Chapter 2 we mentioned the practical constraints arising from the proposed allocation of functions. We therefore see the need for arrangements such as participation of both regional and district staff in relevant programme area teams and the need for joint liaison committees of elected members.

5.25 We are conscious of the enormous burdens which will be placed on elected members and officers of all authorities in the transitional period of reorganisation and we recognise that certain fundamental matters, particularly the preservation of a continuing high level of service to the public must be foremost. We are, however, totally convinced of the importance of the corporate approach in ensuring the future well-being of the public in Scotland and we commend the new authorities most strongly to set about the task with urgency and commitment.

Chapter 6

The service functions

Introduction

6.1   In earlier chapters we set out the basic principles which in our view should be adopted by the new authorities in determining their forms of organisation. We outlined the key elements of a corporate structure and illustrated how the corporate system might operate. As we said in Chapter 1, structures of themselves are meaningless unless they are related to the tasks which have to be undertaken and are tailored to permit the most effective provision of the services required by the public. We have therefore taken a close look at the services provided by local authorities in order to assess the practical implications in terms of possible structures. We included in our review not only those services which are direct providers, such as education and housing (which we examine in this chapter), but also the central services such as finance and architecture which support them (Chapter 7).

6.2   We considered the main operational tasks and processes within each of the services and functions, the links between services and the links with the public, particularly those in which the public themselves are the initiators. We were greatly assisted in our task by the evidence submitted to us by the professional associations and by the information received from joint advisory committees and their working parties.

6.3   In examining the workings of the various services, we have had to restrain our inclination to delve too deeply into detail since our task was not to write a treatise on each service. In the body of the report, therefore, we have confined our comments to the more important aspects and have illustrated in Appendix 12 how the main elements of the important regional and islands functions might be allocated as between headquarters and more locally based units.

6.4 In our consultations with the professional associations we particularly asked for their views on what objective yardsticks could be used to define the optimum size of locally based units for their own functions. The associations gave careful consideration to this request but in most cases they felt that the wide variation in local circumstances throughout the country made it virtually impossible to specify criteria which would be universally applicable.

6.5 It is important to recognise the linkages which exist between functions, not only those which are the responsibility of the same tier (such as education and social work) but also those which are allocated to different tiers (such as social work and housing) or are concurrent (such as recreation and leisure). Furthermore, we have been struck by the frequency with which the same principles or considerations seemed to be common to many functions. We have therefore set out the sections of this chapter not by strict subdivision into regional or district responsibilities but have, in certain cases, considered together functions which appeared to have the strongest linkages. We separate them later in Chapter 8 when making specific structural proposals for the different authorities.

6.6 The constraints created by the allocation of related services to different levels are of course not relevant in the case of the islands authorities, although the requirements for inter-departmental co-operation and local devolution still apply. When we refer to these latter requirements in a regional context, therefore, our remarks should also be read as applicable to the islands.

The personal services—education, social work and housing

6.7 We look first at education, social work and housing, all of which are pre-eminently concerned with individuals and groups of people within the community. Consequently they have much in common in the nature of the job they have to do and the kind of organisation they need to do it. A major factor in the effectiveness of these services is the local organisations whose basic components are the operational units such as schools, community centres, social worker field teams, residential care establishments and local housing offices. These operational units need support. For housing this would be provided from the district headquarters. In the case of education and social work, sub-regional management units would also be required. In Strathclyde the size of the task may be such that a further level of control between the sub-regions and headquarters would be needed.

6.8 Broadly we see the headquarters units being concerned with assessment of need and formulation of policy, planning of provision and monitoring of implementation. Headquarters would lay down professional and administrative guide-lines and provide specialist or advisory services on such matters as care of the homeless, family casework problems, education advisory services and child guidance. In some cases the headquarters unit would also undertake the management of certain facilities and establishments with a wide catchment area, for instance a sheltered workshop or a special education unit for handicapped children. The sub-regional units would undertake the detailed administration of services, decisions being taken within the framework of the policy laid down centrally. Examples of the possible division of tasks are given in Appendix 12.

6.9 Education and social work have links at both headquarters and operational levels through such matters as mutual referrals of pupils and families, special education, pre-school provision, the social welfare aspects of education and the youth and community service. Other services—such as libraries, museums and art galleries, recreation, physical training—have links with education through a mutual concern for the development of a leisure and recreation programme and in the common use of buildings, staff and other facilities for recreation purposes.

6.10 As far as social work is concerned, the link with housing stands out as being of major importance. At the policy planning level there is common concern for the social environment and amenity of housing developments and the provision of sheltered housing. At the operational level social workers in the field are concerned with the support of families whose difficulties may be bound up with housing conditions and the consequences of housing policy.

6.11 Housing has many links apart from that with social work. In the case of new housing, for instance, roads, traffic management, drainage and water services are an integral part of the development. The lighting service maintains stair and high-rise flat lighting and undertakes general electrical work in houses. Housing also has links with the sanitary services.

6.12 In all of the personal services a significant link is the local contact with individuals and families and with professional, governmental and voluntary bodies in the community.

6.13 All of the links identified fall into two basic categories—those existing between services and those relating to contact with the public. We now consider how these links might be fostered.

6.14 We referred in Chapter 5 to the possible combining of departments which have closely related objectives. However, in the case of these major personal services, we do not consider a permanent grouping of departments to be a practical proposition except perhaps for those tasks related to leisure and recreation which we discuss later in this chapter.

6.15 This being the case, we must consider other working arrangements. These might take some or all of the following forms:

△ consultation between elected members of region and district perhaps in the shape of a liaison committee; this same committee could consider all matters of mutual interest and concern, not merely the personal services

△ in the larger regions, area committees of regional members with general oversight of devolved regional functions; such committees could deal with issues which are sensitive and important locally but which do not materially affect overall regional policy; extreme care, however, will be required in framing their precise remit in order to avoid fragmentation of policy and inconsistency of application; in Strathclyde, because of the special requirements of the Bill in respect of education and social work (Clause 56), it may be desirable to reflect the devolved officer structure also in the member arrangements

△ close contact between district officers and the relevant officers of the region

△ the participation of both regional and district officers in relevant programme area or project teams

△ finally, there is the close co-ordination which should be achieved at headquarters level between the policy and resources committees and the chief executives and their management teams.

6.16   The second category of link is that with the public. In view of the close links between education, social work and housing at the community level and the fact that all of these services may come together to deal with one family, we recommend that the sub-regional boundaries of education and social work should coincide with one or more district boundaries and that the sub-regional offices of education and social work and the district housing office be at or near the same location. At this point we emphasise the importance which we attach to the development in the new authorities of the 'one door' approach to facilitate contact between the public and the authority. We recommend the setting up of general offices at convenient local points to allow members of the public wishing information or assistance from any of the local authority services to have their requests dealt with speedily and effectively. This will entail the manning of these offices with staff possessing wide general knowledge and experience. We think that the provision of this facility should be given high priority irrespective of whether the sub-regional and district offices can be located together in the short term.

6.17   In housing, the field of public contact is much wider than merely routine landlord/tenant relationships. It is becoming generally accepted that a housing authority should be concerned with housing in its widest community sense with involvement in conservation, improvement and home loans and in the private as well as the public sector. We endorse the need, particularly in urban areas, for a housing advisory service capable of dealing with the total range of housing enquiries from all sections of the community. In response to SDD Circular No. 118/1972, Glasgow has already set up such a service and Edinburgh, we understand, is also about to do so. We would commend other districts which are mainly urban to adopt this practice.

6.18   In terms of formal committee arrangements, each region and islands authority must have an education committee and a social work committee. In certain cases, particularly in larger regions, there will probably be a need for standing sub-committees although we feel these should be kept to a minimum. The remit to these standing committees, to area committees and, in the case of education, to the school and college councils will be a matter for each authority to decide.

6.19   In the case of housing, while there is no statutory obligation, it is, we feel, obvious that every district will require to have a housing committee.

Engineering and technical services

6.20 A major responsibility of the new regional and islands authorities will be to provide roads, lighting, sewerage and water services, all of which have a significant impact on the life of a community; roads are an integral part of living in town and country; lighting has safety and amenity importance; efficient drainage and sewerage systems are vital to health; water is an essential element in home and industry.

6.21 There is common ground between the engineering services. In the first place they are concerned with the environment in forming the physical pattern for area and community development. In the second place there is a common concern with the practicalities of engineering—such as the design, construction and maintenance of roads, sewers and sewage treatment plants, water installations and lighting systems.

6.22 The engineering services will be administered over broad geographic areas with widely varying needs. An important feature of the structure of these services is again the local organisation. The local organisation for roads, sewerage, water and lighting functions is no less important than that for the personal services. There is a need for an effective sub-regional organisation for the following reasons:

△ services should be provided as close as possible to the place of need; for instance the repair and maintenance of roads and sewers is essentially a local matter and is likely to be undertaken by local labour forces or local contractors

△ the engineering services have close links with housing as already indicated

△ the resources of manpower, plant, equipment and materials must be effectively deployed and controlled

△ a point of ready public access is needed; members of the public require information and their requests and griev-ances must be dealt with promptly; industrialists, developers, private firms of architects and builders all need technical information and advice from the engineering services.

6.23 The basic components of the local organisations are the operational units such as construction and maintenance work forces, depots, reservoirs and sewage treatment plants. These operational units need support from sub-regional organisations and head-quarters units. In their report the Scottish Engineering Group express the view that in the case of Strathclyde the scope and scale of operations and the geographic spread of the area will require the creation of an intermediate level of control between sub-regions and headquarters.

6.24 We now look at the structural implications of the linkages between the various engineering and technical services. We have already noted the common ground between them at the policy planning level and the similarity in their general organisational and technical requirements. Within many existing authorities this fact has been recognised and engineering services have undergone some degree of grouping. In the case of the new authorities, the engineering professional associations have put forward various grouping pro-posals. The possibilities appear to us to be as follows:

△   roads, sewerage and water grouped in one department

△   roads as a separate department, and sewerage and water combined in a water services department

△   roads, sewerage and water as separate departments.

The scale of operations and geography of each region will determine which of these possibilities is most suitable. The first alternative, for example, could be appropriate in the smaller regions and in the islands authorities, whereas the third alternative could be necessary in Strathclyde.

6.25 The headquarters level of these services would be concerned with the assessment of need; the formulation of policy; the develop-ment of programmes, technical standards and administrative guide-lines; the setting up of co-ordination machinery between disciplines; and the provision of specialist services in, for instance, design, traffic management and sewage treatment. The involvement of roads engineers in the important matter of transportation policy is dis-cussed below (paragraphs 6.32–6.33). Sub-regions would be con-cerned with the implementation of agreed policy and with the day-to-day management of operations—deployment and supervision of labour forces, deployment of plant and materials and the organisation of the necessary technical and administrative support services. They would also provide the link with the public.

6.26 Apart from links between the engineering services themselves, there are also the links with other regional and district services and with the public. The roads service through its responsibility for road safety, parking and traffic management matters generally has links with local planning and with the police. Roads may also link with cleansing on matters of road and street cleaning, and on weather emergency operations. The sewerage and drainage services are involved in building control and with environmental health. We have already mentioned the links which all of the technical services have with housing.

6.27 It has been put to us that there may be a case for setting up district engineering services departments because of:

△ the close involvement in new housing developments of the main engineering disciplines already referred to, and

△ the need, in other district functions, for specialist engineering assistance such as structural engineering in architecture and building control.

We do not consider, however, that these reasons justify the creation of a district engineering department except perhaps in the largest districts. Elsewhere, while we see certain specialists being employed in user departments, we envisage districts obtaining any other necessary engineering services from the region on an agency basis or from private consultants.

6.28 The links with the community are of three types. Firstly, any member of the general public may wish to contact the roads, sewerage or water services on a variety of matters such as the state of repair of local roads and footpaths; local problems raised by car parking, road safety and traffic management schemes and drainage and water emergencies or complaints. The second link is with developers; major developments will involve extensive discussion of both engineering and planning matters and there will require to be a close tie-in with the procedure for dealing with planning applications. The third type of link is with private firms of engineers and architects and with builders, all of whom require technical information, advice and general assistance.

6.29 Our consideration of these links leads us to conclude that the same arrangements apply to the engineering services as have already been discussed in paragraph 6.15 in respect of the personal services and we do not re-state them here. Our comments on the location of local offices are also applicable.

6.30 We consider that the boundaries of the engineering sub-regional units should be co-terminous with one or more districts. However, in the case of drainage and water, we recognise that hydrological considerations may necessitate some departure from this pattern. We would also urge public undertakings to revise their operational boundaries to coincide with the new local authority areas.

6.31 There are three particular aspects of the engineering and technical services which require further elaboration. These are highway planning and transportation, lighting and specialist engineering services. These we now discuss.

6.32 In our earlier remarks about roads, we concentrated our attention on the design, construction and maintenance of roads at the stage when the tasks are essentially engineering ones. However, as also emphasised earlier, the engineering services play an important part in the formation of the physical environment. This is of particular relevance in the case of highway planning and transportation planning, both of which have a significant engineering content but which at the same time are integral to land-use planning.

6.33 In the submissions made to us, highway planning, transportation planning and land use planning were often mentioned together and differing views were expressed as to whether the physical planner or the engineer should be responsible. From our own examination of the tasks involved we have concluded that the engineering and planning elements are inextricably intermeshed and that the engineers and planners must work together in the closest partnership. It appears impracticable that all the disciplines necessary to carry out this and related planning tasks should be permanently located in one department. We therefore envisage the setting up of a multi-disciplinary programme area team whose members would be drawn as required from the relevant departments.

6.34 In the few authorities which have substantial public transport undertakings of their own, we would foresee the operational management task being carried out by a separate department (in Strathclyde's case, the Passenger Transport Executive) with representation on the transportation programme area team.

6.35 Lighting has close affinities with roads, being concerned with the installation and maintenance of roads lighting and with the lighting of traffic signals and signs. It is also akin to a specialist central service in some authorities, being called upon to carry out work for, or provide an advisory service to, any department with electrical installations. While there will be a substantial lighting task in the regions, there are also district lighting requirements in areas such as stairs and footpaths. The question arises as to whether lighting should be totally a regional responsibility, providing a service to district authorities on an agency basis, or whether there should also be a district lighting service. The Association of Public Lighting Engineers—critical of the present fragmented nature of lighting services—takes the view that lighting is concerned with developing technology requiring highly trained staff, specialist equipment and methods, and that the opportunity should now be taken to obtain the advantage of economies of scale. The Association concludes that lighting should be a totally regional service and should carry out work on an agency basis for districts. We accept this view since a split in the service would be wasteful of resources and could raise technical and administrative difficulties. We foresee the lighting service being a section of the roads department.

6.36 It has been suggested that there should be in the new authorities a central engineering advisory service to meet the demand for specialist expertise in such disciplines as structural, heating and ventilating and electrical engineering. On balance, however, we consider that such specialists should be located within those departments having a continuing requirement for them and that they should be available to give advice elsewhere in the authority. Individual requirements of the new authorities will dictate their optimum location.

44

6.37 In terms of formal committee arrangements for the engineering and technical services, a similar number of possibilities exists as with departments. In certain regions and in the islands authorities it would be feasible to have one committee responsible for all of the services considered in this section of the report. In others there could be justification for two committees, or perhaps two sub-committees of one parent committee dealing respectively with roads and with water services, including sewerage. In Strathclyde it will probably be necessary to set up three committees or three sub-committees of one parent committee, to cover roads, sewerage and water separately. In those regions with sizeable public transport responsibilities it may also be necessary to have a separate committee or sub-committee for this function. In Strathclyde this committee would be responsible for most of the activities of the former Passenger Transport Authority although the major strategic matters should come within the purview of the policy and resources committee.

Physical planning

6.38 In Chapter 5 we drew the distinction between policy planning —which is the unified planning process at the core of the authority's corporate management system—and the planning carried out under existing town and country planning legislation. We emphasise that it is the latter which we now consider in this section of the report; to avoid confusion we refer to it as physical planning.

6.39 The main tasks involved in physical planning are:

△   the land-use aspects of the structure plans (regions) and local plans including urban development and the country-side (districts and general planning authorities)

△   the planning of development, including industrial development and tourism

△   development control.

6.40 In their submission to us, the County Planning Officers' Society for Scotland emphasised the continuity of the planning process from the strategic level at one end of the spectrum to the local level at the other. We agree with this view. Where the responsibility for planning is divided between region and districts,

45

therefore, there are significant organisational implications since in practice the two levels must work as one in order to prepare physical plans and to implement them. The challenge facing the new authorities is a practical one. The work and investment of the two planning levels must be co-ordinated on the ground, and regional and district authorities will have to work jointly on such matters as industrial development, countryside facilities and recreational open space. It is clear to us that there is a requirement for joint working arrangements of officers from region and districts on a continuing basis, although we do not see (except in the general planning authorities) the same requirement for permanent outposting of regional staff as we do in the case of the personal and engineering services already discussed. We have already emphasised the need for liaison arrangements at member level between region and districts covering all matters of mutual concern and we feel that the arrangement is particularly vital in the case of physical planning. In the early period after reorganisation, before structure plans have been prepared, it is possible that the volume of planning matters to be considered jointly could be substantial, in which case special provisions may be required. We do not, however, see this as a continuing requirement in the longer term.

6.41 Development control represents an important point of contact between the authority and the local community. Except in general planning authorities it is a district responsibility. Certain applications, however, will have to be considered by the regional planning authority and, where policy had not been clearly defined, may have to be referred to the policy and resources committee for decision. It is therefore essential that region and district should co-operate in setting up effective machinery for dealing with planning applications.

6.42 In this connection we also recommend that the new authorities, to assist members of the public, should set up an integrated system for handling applications for planning and building control permissions.

6.43 There will be a requirement for a committee at both region and district levels to take responsibility for the physical planning function. However, because of the very close link with policy planning, we think there should be a linked arrangement between the policy and resources committee and the planning and development committee whose remit should be concerned with the land use aspects of structure and/or local plans and with development control.

6.44 In certain authorities there could be a requirement for separate committee arrangements to deal with the implementation of particular plans covering, for example, industrial or tourist development. The need for these can only be gauged in the light of particular local circumstances.

Leisure and recreation

6.45 In this section we consider a range of functions which together constitute a very important sector of local government activity. The range covers libraries, museums, theatres, swimming pools, other physical recreation facilities, community centres, halls, parks and play spaces.

6.46 The various submissions made to us emphasise the accelerating interest in and demand for recreation, leisure and sporting facilities. Consequently there is increasing pressure from many quarters for a greatly extended and co-ordinated provision over the whole field. Within existing authorities planning and provision is fragmented and consequently there are many inadequacies. The fear has been expressed to us, by those working in this field, that after reorganisation the present shortcomings could be perpetuated or even accentuated since, with the exception of libraries, both levels of local government will have a joint responsibility for recreation and culture. We agree that the danger is a real one.

6.47 Broadly, the tasks to be undertaken are assessment of need, formulation of policy and the provision and management of facilities. We see the assessment of local needs being undertaken at district level, the region being responsible for obtaining the necessary information from districts to satisfy itself that the overall need is being met. We see the region and districts working together in overall policy matters and in the planning of provision within which there would be scope for the development of local policy and local priorities. In this context the region would have close links with the regional sports council and cultural bodies; the district would have liaison with local sports councils, clubs and other groups in the community. Both authorities would be concerned to maintain close links with the many voluntary organisations which supplement the local authority provision to a considerable extent. We see the district authority as the principal provider and manager of facilities although we would expect the region to be responsible at least for the provision, if not necessarily for the day-to-day management, of facilities with an obviously regional significance. The region might also be expected to assist in cases where districts have clearly established a need for certain facilities but are unable to provide these entirely from their own resources.

6.48 A major complication in achieving the degree of integration we feel desirable is the long association of youth and community work and certain cultural provisions with the education service. Much of the evidence we have received from educational sources has stressed the undesirability and the practical difficulties of disrupting present arrangements, particularly those concerned with the deployment of staff. There is also the question of the use of community facilities in educational buildings.

6.49 We have noted that the Select Committee of the House of Lords on Sport and Leisure have recommended in their first report that each region should set up a department of recreation with its own chief officer and should also set up a recreation committee. The submissions which we have received from organisations such as the Scottish Sports Council and the Institute of Park and Recreation Administration make similar recommendations. We have no hesitation in endorsing these recommendations.

6.50 At district level we also consider that a committee for leisure and recreation is essential. On the officer side, however, the issue is less clear cut. The possibilities appear to be as follows:

△ the creation of a single directorate covering all aspects of leisure and recreation in accordance with the programme area concept

△ the creation of one department responsible for all aspects of physical recreation, including parks and a separate department for cultural aspects such as libraries and museums

△ the creation of independent departments or sections for each or most of the various activities, leaving co-ordination to be achieved through the leisure and recreation committee and the chief executive.

The main argument against the ideal first approach is that from the practical management standpoint, physical recreation and cultural activities each require quite different knowledge and expertise. To a lesser extent the same argument is used against the second approach because of the different types of specialist knowledge claimed to be required even within each of these two spheres.

6.51 We accept the practical argument against the first approach and favour instead the setting up in most districts of separate departments for physical recreation and for libraries and museums respectively. While it is claimed that there is at present a shortage of managers suitably qualified across the whole range of physical recreation activities, we understand that steps are now being taken in national training programmes to fill this gap. The short-term deficiency therefore should not be allowed to preclude the adoption of an otherwise desirable arrangement.

6.52 In the smaller districts it is likely that the scale of activities would not justify the appointment of a head of recreation. In these cases the individual section heads, such as parks superintendents and baths managers, would each report to the chief executive.

6.53 We are advised that the smaller districts would find it difficult to provide a comprehensive library service and furthermore that the existing level of service could be seriously impaired by the fragmentation of the present county library arrangements. We would therefore suggest that such districts should give serious consideration to the possibility of joint arrangements.

6.54 By now we have probably stressed sufficiently the need for co-operation between region and district. In this area of concurrent responsibility the need is underlined more forcibly—particularly with the requirement for early definition of respective responsibilities —and most of the joint arrangements previously outlined should be applicable in this case. We also emphasise the requirement for close co-operation and involvement with outside bodies such as the Scottish Sports Council, the Countryside Commission and with other voluntary bodies involved in the recreation and leisure sphere.

Consumer protection

6.55 Under this heading we consider the regional responsibility for trading standards, for food standards and labelling and for diseases of animals. These functions have much in common, being concerned with regulatory and enforcement tasks in respect of relevant statutes and require similar types of organisation. We see the structural organisation of these services broadly following the existing county pattern, a view also held by the professional associations. We envisage, therefore, a regional headquarters and a number of sub-regional units staffed by inspectors undertaking local inspection, reporting and advisory functions, giving advice to traders and others and dealing with complaints. The sub-regional boundaries would be dictated by geography and the size of the local task, and the units would consist of inspectors and clerical staff. Here again, for the convenience of the public there would be an advantage if the local offices were in or near to the district offices. The headquarters unit would be mainly concerned with the provision and use of facilities and equipment and the deployment of staff at the local level.

6.56 The nature of the tasks allows these services to be largely self-contained and the necessary links with the public analyst and with the district sanitary services should be adequately maintained by administrative systems.

6.57 We have noted the growing pressure in Parliament and elsewhere for the provision of consumer advice centres, at least in the more densely populated areas, from which the public can obtain advice on a whole range of matters not all of which fall within the authority's direct control. We are aware that such centres already exist, for example in East Kilbride and in several English authorities, and that they receive financial support from the local authority. In principle we are in favour of such a facility. However, we have been unable to devote sufficient attention to the possible detailed implications and arrangements and would commend the matter to the new authorities themselves as worthy of further consideration.

6.58 We consider that all regions will require separate committees and departments responsible for consumer protection.

Environmental health

6.59 Under this heading we discuss the district functions of cleansing, sanitary services, markets and slaughterhouses, all of which have a common concern with health.

6.60 The cleansing service is characterised by the need to manage a sizeable direct labour organisation and fleet of vehicles to carry out cleansing and refuse collection. The other main task is refuse disposal, the technological complexity and costs of which suggest that joint arrangements between smaller districts could be desirable. Cleansing may have links with the roads service and on an agency basis may undertake road sweeping, gulley emptying and weather emergency operations. There are also links with the public in dealing with enquiries and complaints. We do not foresee a need for a sub-district management organisation in cleansing although the operational task will be organised on the basis of local depots, workshops and disposal points.

6.61 The sanitary service is basically an enforcement and protection function and in the nature of its organisation is similar to the consumer protection functions discussed earlier. In geographically large districts there will be a need to establish outposts from which staff would carry out inspections and tests, give advice to traders and deal with enquiries and complaints from the public. At district level there are links with housing, both public and private, and with markets and slaughterhouses where these exist. There are also links at regional level with such functions as trading standards, food standards and labelling and with the public analyst as already mentioned. In certain cases it may be convenient for the sanitary service to undertake some regional consumer protection tasks on an agency basis.

6.62 At elected member level we consider that an environmental health committee should be responsible for all of the functions discussed in this section. On the officer side, however, we consider that the common concern for health already noted is outweighed by the essential differences in the nature of the operational tasks of cleansing and sanitary services. We do not therefore see a combination of these departments as being necessary or desirable except in the smaller districts.

51

Building control

6.63 Building control is a regulatory and enforcement function arising out of the application of the Building Regulations. The organisation is of the inspectorate type which we have already seen in the sanitary services. The main tasks include the preparation of reports on applications for building warrants, the amendment of plans, site inspections and the deployment of inspectorate staff.

6.64 There are links with the public including enquiries from professional firms and property owners and technical discussions with major developers or their agents. As already indicated, one of the most important internal links is with physical planning because of the close administrative tie-up of the procedures dealing with applications for planning permission and building permission. There are also links with the fire service and with legal and sanitary services in respect of enforcement action.

6.65 It has been put to us that building control could be grouped with the sanitary service or with physical planning. In existing authorities we found a number of ad hoc arrangements, not all of which were satisfactory. In the new authorities we have no doubt that building control should be grouped with physical planning because of the strong links between them. On any occasion when structural engineering expertise is required in a depth not normally available in the building control section, this should be obtained, as already suggested, from the engineering services.

6.66 In general planning authorities, building control is a regional responsibility and in such cases there will be a requirement for outposts to provide a base for inspectors and a point of contact for the public.

6.67 At elected member level, responsibility should lie with the planning and development committee. Since applications for planning and for building permissions are essentially two separate processes from the legal standpoint, it is probably desirable in practice to process applications through two sub-committees of the planning and development committee.

Police and fire services

6.68 The uniformed services enjoy more operational freedom than other functions but have nevertheless important links with certain other local authority services. For example, the police work closely with children's panels and with traffic management, road safety, licensing and diseases of animals functions. The fire service has important links with building control and with other departments concerned with the implementation of fire regulations.

6.69 Police offices and fire stations are located strategically throughout communities and public contact does not appear to present any difficulty.

6.70 Within the regions the police and fire services will require to create a divisional structure for operational control. We think it would be advantageous if these divisional boundaries coincided wherever possible with the sub-regional boundaries of other services.

6.71 At elected member level these services should be the responsibility of a police and fire committee except in those regions and the islands authorities where separate joint committees are to be set up. The appointment of chief constables and firemasters is mandatory.

The assessor

6.72 The lands valuation assessor is not subject to the control of the local authority as far as his main task of valuation is concerned. However, he has certain links such as with the chief finance officer on rating matters and, in his capacity as electoral registration officer, with the clerk. In addition the assessor's department holds much basic data which will form an important part of the authority's comprehensive information system which we advocated in Chapter 5. The estates function, which is partially undertaken in some authorities by the assessor, is discussed separately in Chapter 7. In terms of the public's contact with the assessor there will be a need for local offices along the lines currently provided.

6.73 In the new authorities the assessor retains his independent status but we foresee no problems in preserving the necessary links with other local authority departments by administrative means.

Common features of the services

6.74 We have now considered the service functions and their main tasks and links. Apart from the organisational aspects particular to each service (which we incorporate in our recommendations in Chapter 8), there are two common features emerging which require to be underlined.

6.75 The first is the necessity for the local organisation which is a fundamental requirement in providing effective service. Thus we see an extensive devolution of the major regional services, ideally to locations in close proximity with each other and with the district services and having the same sub-regional boundaries co-terminous with districts or groups of districts. In geographically large districts devolution will also be required.

6.76 In Chapter 4 we emphasised the need for decisions to be taken at the lowest level of the organisation consistent with the nature of the problem. If the local units are to be effective we are in no doubt that they must be true units of management, the officers in charge being recognised as accountable for the areas concerned within the terms of reference allocated to them by the regional council and committees. The units should also act as the important sensory mechanism for interpreting and communicating local needs. It would defeat the objectives of the sub-regional structure as we envisage it if the units became no more than reporting points and agencies for referring all matters and complaints upwards to headquarters for decision.

6.77 The second feature is the sheer number and extent of the detailed linkages which have been identified. This highlights even more strongly the need for the corporate approach not only at the top level but throughout the whole organisation, and we have therefore indicated (for example in paragraph 6.15) possible arrangements which might be adopted.

6.78 Before concluding this chapter we feel we should comment on a particular suggestion which has been made regarding the overall co-ordination of devolved regional services within a particular area —that this should be achieved through the appointment of a senior officer akin almost to a mini-chief executive. While we concede that such co-ordination is important, we believe that it can best be achieved by the measures already outlined. We do not favour the creation of such a post because it would in our view impair the authority of the chief officers, create difficulties of control and possibly lead to inconsistencies of approach throughout the region.

Chapter 7

The central support functions

Introduction

7.1   In this chapter we consider those functions which support the top management structure and the service departments, assisting them to carry out their tasks effectively and efficiently. The functions we discuss are finance, personnel, management services, computer, architecture, legal services, administration, services to members, estates, public relations, supplies, internal transport, property maintenance, and common office services.

7.2   Collectively these form a core of administrative, specialist and advisory expertise serving all the departments of the authority. The objectives of centralising certain services are to achieve a better integration of the management process and in certain cases to achieve a fuller utilisation of specialist skills. We would emphasise, however, that centralisation is not an end in itself and we have kept this in mind in our examination of the central support functions.

Finance

7.3   We identify two main divisions of financial tasks. First, there is the forward planning role which is concerned with the financing of the authority's policy plan and with the financial evaluation of the service programmes and alternatives. The importance of financial forward planning in the management of an authority's affairs cannot be over-emphasised and although it is being carried out on an increasing scale the processes still need much development. Second, there is the management of the on-going financial tasks such as loans and debt administration, income and expenditure, investment, internal audit, management accounting and financial information systems. This aspect of the finance function is already well developed although we would draw attention to the substantial task of management of their loans funds which will face the new district authorities.

7.4 Finance is an integral part of the management process and therefore all departments of an authority will to some extent carry on financial operations although they should do so within the framework laid down by a central finance department. For example, service departments would operate systems connected with departmental accounts including costing, supplies and stores book-keeping, passing accounts for payment and preparation of information for payment of wages. In the case of regional services we see such tasks being undertaken at the local management level where much of the basic information necessary for financial purposes originates.

7.5 The scope and scale of any particular service function will largely determine the degree of development of the finance function within that service and, in turn, the level of financial expertise necessary. In a large regional service it is likely that there will be a well developed finance function probably to the extent of a requirement for qualified accountants on the staff. In such cases we do not see the permanent secondment of accounting staff from a central finance service to a service department as being a satisfactory arrangement from a management point of view. However, we do envisage the necessity for staff in the central finance service to be outposted to service departments for limited periods to undertake special investigations. The service departments would also be able to call for special assistance from the central finance service as required. In smaller authorities where the scope of certain services is limited, most of the financial tasks would be undertaken centrally.

7.6 We have already said in Chapter 6 that Strathclyde presents a particular challenge to the services from the point of view of devolution of responsibility to the local level. The same consideration may also suggest a need to decentralise certain aspects of the finance function to a local level. Some regional authorities may wish to make an agency arrangement with district authorities for cash collection and minor payments.

7.7 The chief financial officer will be an important member of the executive office as we discuss later in Chapter 8.

Personnel

7.8 As in the case of finance, we identify two main divisions of personnel tasks. First, there is the role of the personnel function in forward planning. Manpower planning is concerned with the formulation and implementation of a policy designed to ensure the availability of the staff required, in terms of quantity and quality, to implement the authority's forward programmes. Little, if any, manpower planning has been carried on in local authorities up to the present time, partly because of the practical difficulties involved in any forward planning in local government. Nevertheless we consider that forward planning generally, and manpower planning's part in it, must be further developed. Second there is the management of the on-going personnel tasks concerned with the formulation and implementation of the authority's personnel policy. This includes advice on staff development and training and on salary and wage structures, the correct application of scales and conditions of employment, negotiations with trade unions and staff associations, fostering of good industrial relations, the development of a recruitment policy, advice on selection procedures, dismissals and redundancies and on disciplinary and grading appeal procedures.

7.9 Many of the tasks which would be the responsibility of a personnel officer are being undertaken to varying degrees of effectiveness in existing local authorities. Hitherto the main concern has been with controlling staff numbers and gradings—'the watchdog' function. While this is important we consider that more emphasis should be placed on the positive aspects of personnel management such as effective staff development and economic deployment of manpower, with the full participation of all department heads. The personnel officer will be closely involved in the plan formulation stage and thereafter in advising how to meet the manpower need in relation to agreed programme requirements.

7.10 Regions, islands and the larger districts will require a high level of expertise in personnel matters necessitating in many cases the appointment of a qualified head of personnel. The smaller districts on the other hand will probably find an administrative officer with personnel training and experience adequate. Personnel matters, like finance, are an integral part of the management process and therefore all departments of an authority will undertake certain personnel tasks for themselves. However, they should be undertaken within the framework laid down centrally. For instance service departments would operate systems concerned with selection, placement and dismissal of staff, certain aspects of training and industrial relations and enquiries on salaries and wages. In the case of regional services we see certain of these tasks or aspects of them being carried out at the local management level.

7.11 As we have already indicated, the scope and scale of the service will determine the general level of personnel operations in the user departments and the level of personnel expertise necessary. The pattern will vary considerably from region to region and from service to service. For example, the personnel units in the larger departments would probably have considerable autonomy and expertise and would carry out their own selection and staff development programmes.

7.12 In our view the personnel function should not be combined with any other support service except in the smaller regions and districts where a grouping with, for example, management services could be considered. There has been much discussion as to whether a grouping of personnel and management services should be a standard organisational pattern. On balance we think the functions should be separate except in the smaller authorities. We see it as essential, however, that there is a close partnership between personnel and management services since they complement one another in a number of areas. The necessary co-ordination should be achieved through the executive office.

7.13 We think that the head of personnel should be regarded as a principal adviser to the chief executive and the management team rather than as an independent chief officer, his reporting line being through the executive office.

Management services

7.14 Management services is the term generally used to describe a number of techniques and specialisms including organisation and methods, work study, operational research and project co-ordination, all of these being readily recognisable as providing analytical or problem solving tools for management.

7.15 Management services have already contributed to improved effectiveness in many sectors of local government, and there is still significant scope for further development in this field. We agree, however, with the point made in many submissions to us that management services should be regarded as an aid to management and not a substitute for it.

7.16 The larger regions and the city districts should be able to support a comprehensive range of management services. Most other districts and the islands authorities would be able to support a work study service but might have to make joint arrangements or employ outside assistance for other specialisms.

7.17 Except in the larger regions the service departments would probably not require their own management services staff apart from work study. In departments such as cleansing, engineering and parks which are major employers of manual staff, there will be a continuing requirement for work study personnel. We see the service department head being responsible for their day-to-day control and the head of central management services being responsible for laying down codes of practice, maintaining professional standards, and instituting any necessary training.

7.18 It has been suggested that organisation and methods and work study could be regarded as separate services. We do not support this view since we believe that the same analytical skills are applicable to both. Present trends indicate that the importance of work study might decrease somewhat with a possible move away from incentive schemes to, for example, high day rate methods of payment. This could highlight the need for the work study practitioner's skill to be utilised in other directions such as methods and systems investigations.

7.19 In terms of possible organisation the considerations already advanced in the case of personnel (paragraph 7.12) are applicable to management services. We think it is fundamental that the chief executive and the management team should be responsible for organisation and methods, work study, operational research, project co-ordination and other techniques in an overall management sense, deciding the priorities and generally directing, co-ordinating and controlling their activities.

7.20 We would therefore see the head of management services reporting in most authorities to a nominated member of the executive office. In the smaller authorities responsibility for management services and personnel might be combined, with the head reporting to a nominated member of the management team.

Computer services

7.21 The computer has a special place in the structure of an authority because of its important role in the development of information systems and in policy planning. Therefore, although much computer work would be concerned with the routine operations of departments, we are in no doubt that the computer should be regarded as a prime tool of the chief executive and his management team. At present the potential of the computer is not being fully exploited in most local authorities. We think that better decision-making would result if computers were put to more use as data banks and for the analysis of information compiled from regions, districts, central government and other sources. From this point of view we regard it as fundamental that there is the closest partnership between a region and the districts within it. We envisage that the regional authorities would provide the bulk of computer services although the large districts may be able to justify some computer capability. In the immediate post reorganisation period, arrangements in the new authorities will depend to a large extent on the location and current usage of existing computer installations.

7.22 In organisation terms we consider that the computer manager should report to a nominated member of the management team, for example, the head of administration or of finance.

Architectural services

7.23 Within our consideration of architectural services we include not only the design function but also quantity surveying and certain other specialist services connected with building, such as heating and ventilating and electrical engineering.

7.24 In their submission to us the various architectural associations have emphasised their concern not merely for functional effectiveness but also for the aesthetic standards of the built environment. While we do not think this is exclusively their domain, we nevertheless feel that the architectural function does need a degree of independence and should not therefore be combined with either the engineering and technical services or with any other central function, except perhaps in the smaller authorities which may have only a limited architectural capability.

7.25 We see the first role of the architectural services as the provision of a top level design facility to all departments, in which respect it is almost akin to a specialist consultancy service. The second role is that of managing and controlling the authority's building projects. We consider the question of property maintenance later in this chapter.

7.26 In the first role close co-operation with the user departments is vital but has not always been achieved to the required extent. We feel, however, that much of the criticism levelled at architects would be obviated if architectural briefs were more clearly defined by the client departments.

7.27 In our earlier consideration of engineering and technical services we expressed the view that certain specialists should be located in the departments which had most need of them. We consider that there could be a requirement for certain of these skills such as structural, heating and ventilating, and electrical engineering in the architect's department.

7.28 Traditionally, quantity surveying has been regarded as an integral part of the overall architectural service although a small number of authorities have in fact created independent quantity surveying sections. We believe that the quantity surveyor, if he is to exercise his responsibilities properly, requires a fair measure of independence. We are not totally convinced that this necessitates a separate department although we would agree with the view expressed by the Royal Institution of Chartered Surveyors that the surveyor's all-round expertise could be used more extensively, particularly in the sphere of project management.

7.29 We consider that service departments should not have architectural sections. The Royal Incorporation of Architects in Scotland in their submission suggested that there would be a need to create divisional or area architects' offices. We do not think that this will be necessary although we acknowledge the requirement for outpostings from time to time to deal with specific projects.

7.30 All regions will require comprehensive architectural services. The larger districts and the islands authorities will probably be able to justify a more limited architectural function. However, in the smaller districts the volume and variety of architectural work could be too limited or sporadic to support a viable service or to provide interest and a career structure for many architects. In these cases the district authority would require to make joint arrangements with other authorities or employ private architects.

7.31 In most authorities we see the architect reporting direct to the chief executive. In the smaller authorities, with only a limited architectural section, a grouping with other technical services may be desirable.

Legal and administrative services

7.32 The scope of the legal services includes conveyancing, parliamentary work, legal procedures and standing orders, contracts, interpretation of statutes and their application to the work of the authority, court work and licensing and regulation functions. There is also the important administrative task of servicing the council and committees and of providing the common services.

7.33 There are mixed views as to whether the administrative functions, particularly the servicing of meetings, should be incorporated with the legal services. Some authorities have established separate legal departments and claim a resulting overall improvement in effectiveness. On the other hand the need for legal knowledge at the centre of deliberations of a statutory body is considered by some to be important. We see the merits of both points of view and find it difficult to reach a firm conclusion. We believe that in the smaller authorities the economics of the situation and the need to provide an attractive career structure for staff make it necessary to combine the functions. In the larger authorities we have, on balance, a preference for the creation of a separate legal department.

Services to members

7.34 Re-organisation will greatly reduce the number of elected members and will place much heavier responsibilities on many. The effective fulfilment of the managerial and representative roles will make substantial demands on members, and in these circumstances we consider it vital that members are given proper facilities and services to assist them in the effective discharge of their duties. Among the desirable arrangements we include the provision of:

△ offices for committee chairmen and, where appropriate, for party group leaders

△ interviewing rooms, with adequate reception arrangements, both at headquarters and at the main local offices

△ libraries and information rooms

△ assistance with research

△ dictating, typing, copying and other secretarial services

△ adequate telephone facilities.

A few existing authorities have made excellent arrangements along these lines but in many cases services to members are still meagre or non-existent. We recommend that the new authorities, notwithstanding any short-term accommodation difficulties, should give proper consideration to the provision of these essential services.

Estates

7.35 Within existing authorities the extent of development of the estates function varies widely. In many cases estates work is fragmented among several departments such as the clerk's, treasurer's and assessor's, although a few authorities have set up separate estates departments.

7.36 There are two key aspects of the estates function. The first is concerned with the valuation of land and property for the purposes of the authority's transactions as a major owner and developer. This includes work connected with, for example, town centre redevelopment, comprehensive development areas, major road improvements and acquisitions for specific service department requirements. In this aspect there is a close tie-up at present with the district valuer. The second aspect is the business management role, concerned with realising the business potential afforded by the authority's land and property assets. In this field there is an increasing involvement in the promotion of industrial and commercial development.

7.37 In terms of organisational requirements it is difficult to be conclusive on the valuation aspect until the role of the district valuer is clarified following the Government's consideration of the report of the Borner Committee. The second aspect is, however, important in its own right. In the regions and the larger urban districts therefore we consider there is justification for a separate estates section in close proximity to the chief executive and the management team, with its reporting line through the executive office.

Public relations

7.38 Public relations, in as far as they are practised in existing local authorities, are generally the responsibility of the clerk. We consider that effective public relations are of prime importance in bridging the gap between the local authority and members of the public. Indeed we think an increased recognition within local government of the importance of public relations would do much to avoid the general ignorance of the public about their local authorities.

7.39 In addition to the important task of projecting the authority's image and effectively publicising its intentions, public relations should also encompass industrial development publicity and the regular provision of information to the public on a wide variety of general matters including, for example, tourism. During the transitional period, public relations will require to play a particularly important role in ensuring maximum public awareness and knowledge of the effects of reorganisation and also in providing effective communication with local authority staff at all levels.

7.40 We therefore see a need, at least in the larger authorities, for an experienced professional public relations officer. In organisational terms he would be attached to a central administrative department but would require to have ready access to elected members and all departments of the authority.

Supplies

7.41 The main organisational issue surrounding the purchasing and supplies functions is the degree of centralisation or decentralisation which is appropriate. The chief arguments put forward for centralising purchasing in one department are largely economic. For instance there are advantages to be gained by obtaining long-term contracts and in bulk purchase; central buying allows standardisation in the goods bought for the authority and a large central department would contain professional buying expertise. The point is also made that, from the standpoint of accountability, purchasing and consuming should not be carried out in the same department.

7.42 A feature of purchasing in a local authority is the comprehensiveness of the range of goods bought. Each class of goods has its own market of which the purchaser requires some knowledge. Within existing authorities various arrangements exist; in some cases purchasing is largely centralised, in others it is partially centralised for certain classes of goods in the department which either possesses the necessary expertise or is the largest user; another arrangement is to have the administration of purchasing centralised but the specification of goods and suppliers carried out by the user departments.

7.43 Despite the apparent logic of central purchasing and supplies we think that the concept of centralisation should not be slavishly followed. We believe that flexibility in tackling purchasing problems will be essential since local circumstances may well dictate a shift of emphasis towards decentralisation in respect of certain items. We emphasise, however, that an authority should have an overall purchasing policy which builds in all the advantages of centralised purchasing wherever this is practicable.

7.44 The size of the purchasing task in regions and probably the largest districts would warrant the setting up of a centralised purchasing department in some form, perhaps included in a central administrative grouping with finance or administration. Districts could make arrangements to use the purchasing expertise at region and in many cases we think they could use regional contracts to considerable advantage.

Internal transport

7.45 As in purchasing, the main organisational issue concerns centralisation or decentralisation. The arguments supporting centralisation are based on the potential economic benefits of centralised buying and maintenance and on improved utilisation of vehicles. However, there are counter arguments which claim, for example, that centralised arrangements are cumbersome, not necessarily cheaper and too inflexible to meet changing local requirements. It is also claimed that the expertise needed to maintain certain special-purpose vehicles, such as those used in lighting and cleansing, is better provided and controlled within the user department than in a central workshop.

7.46 The optimum arrangement for the organisation of internal transport is a complex question requiring much deeper study than is appropriate in the context of this report. We consider that this question should be determined in the light of particular local circumstances and will, in any case, be largely conditioned in the short term by existing arrangements.

Property maintenance

7.47 Within existing authorities there is a wide variety of arrangements for undertaking property maintenance. These range from a single property maintenance department, responsible for work on all of the authority's properties, to the division of responsibility among different departments for different types of property. An important factor affecting the arrangements is the existence or otherwise of a direct labour department. In the absence of a property maintenance department, the departments most commonly responsible for aspects of maintenance work include works, architect's, engineer's and housing departments.

7.48 In the new authorities several options are available. In the regions, for example, responsibility could be given to the architect, or a central property maintenance department could be set up; there is also the possibility of a region asking districts to carry out maintenance on an agency basis. In the districts the function might be undertaken by the architect, by a works department or by the housing department which is likely to have the greatest maintenance requirements; in the larger districts a central property maintenance department might be justified.

7.49 Any of these possibilities may be valid and the decision can only be made by the new authorities themselves in the light of particular local circumstances and existing arrangements. Whatever pattern is chosen, we would emphasise the need in districts for the close involvement of the housing department since housing maintenance is a key factor in the relationship between tenants and the authority as landlord.

Common office services

7.50 Common office services include telephones, mailing, printing and reprographics, security, messenger services, cleaning, typing pools and catering. The extent to which common office services can be developed depends to a large extent on the geographical location of departments and the ease of communications within and between buildings. Where these permit the setting up of a common services section, its head should be responsible to the head of central administration.

General features

7.51 From our review of the central support function two general points emerge. The first of these concerns the relationship between the central support functions and the service departments. Throughout the report we have advocated the adoption, where practicable, of a programme area approach to organisation, based on objectives rather than functions. The central services, however, are function-rather than objective-oriented; they exist more to provide internal skills than to fulfil the authority's objectives for the community. While we have indicated in this chapter certain specialisms which could be partially located in the service, or programme, departments, practical considerations dictate that in most cases the support functions need to be organised centrally. We emphasise, however, that all of the central functions should be regarded as skills at the disposal of the chief executive and the management team to assist them in achieving their objectives.

7.52 The second point is that there will be a wide variation in the degree of development of individual support functions depending on the size and characteristics of the authority and the scope and scale of their service responsibilities. In the regions and probably in the large districts most of the support functions would be individually identifiable as units or sections although various groupings are possible as already suggested. In smaller authorities functions which have some natural affinity might merge, whilst certain other specialisms might cease to be viable, in which case it would be necessary to consider joint arrangements or to bring in outside assistance.

Chapter 8

Recommended structures for the new authorities

The basic structure

8.1 We have now reached the stage where we have:

△ considered the nature of the proposed reform,

△ sought to establish the need for the corporate approach,

△ described the key features of the corporate structure and outlined possible steps in the corporate management process, and

△ examined the organisational implications of the various service and central support functions.

We proceed now to specific organisational proposals, but first recapitulate the features of the basic corporate structure.

8.2 The basic organisational arrangement which we recommend is illustrated opposite.

8.3 In the committee illustration the linked nature of the resource committees is stressed and in the officer structure the central position of the management team is emphasised.

The executive office

8.4 We have already indicated that the chief executive should not have direct responsibility for a major department except in the smaller authorities; at the same time, however, it is vital to ensure that he does not become isolated but has at his disposal all the necessary facilities to keep himself fully informed and, in particular,

Committee structure

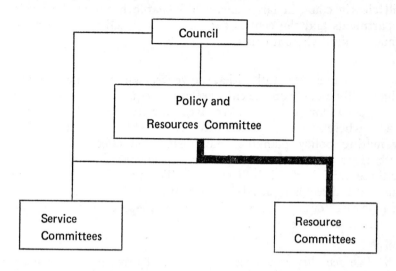

Officer structure

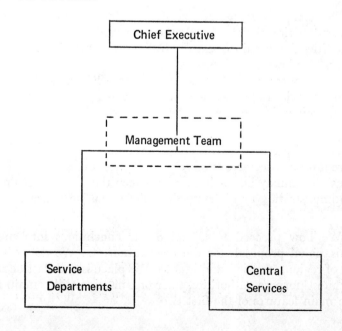

69

to carry out his co-ordinative role in policy planning. His support will clearly come in large measure from the heads of the service departments and the central support services and from the policy planning unit where it exists.

8.5 In the larger authorities, however, the immense demands which will be made on the chief executive require a more formalised arrangement for his support. We favour the concept of the 'executive office' whereby the chief executive is assisted, in his tasks of co-ordinating policy planning, monitoring the effectiveness of the authority's programmes and managing the central services, by two or three officials of chief officer status. These would be a director of finance, a director of administration and, in the largest authorities of all, a director of policy planning. These officers could be designated as depute chief executives.

8.6 We see this as a necessary practical arrangement to ensure that the burdens of the chief executive do not overwhelm him. We would underline strongly, however, that it should not be regarded in any way as diminishing the role of the service department heads in the management team.

8.7 The composition of the executive office is illustrated in the diagram opposite, which also shows the proposed allocation of responsibilities for certain of the central support functions.
The possible allocation of responsibility for other central functions—such as computer, personnel, management services, estates, public relations, purchasing and common services—is less clear cut and is best determined in the light of particular local circumstances.

8.8 We indicate later in this chapter the authorities which we feel may require a director of policy planning. In other authorities his responsibilities may be re-allocated between the directors of finance and administration or direct to the chief executive himself.

8.9 We now proceed to assemble our conclusions into specific organisational proposals for the new authorities. We do so in the order of regions, districts and islands. We place islands last because, being most-purpose authorities, their organisation will contain most of the main features of the first two.

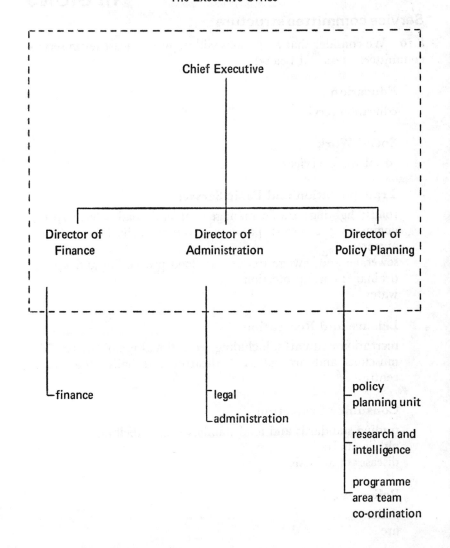

Chief Executive

Director of
Finance

Director of
Administration

Director of
Policy Planning

finance

legal
administration

policy
planning unit

research and
intelligence

programme
area team
co-ordination

Service committee structure

8.10 We consider that all regions will require at least seven service committees as set out below:

Education

education services

Social Work

social work services

Transportation and Basic Services

roads; lighting; traffic management and road safety; special engineering services; passenger transport, harbour services, airports

sewerage and sewage treatment; flood prevention and arterial drainage; coast protection

water

Leisure and Recreation

recreation and parks, including recreational use of countryside; museums and art galleries; theatres and halls; community centres

Consumer Protection

trading standards and food standards and labelling
public analyst
diseases of animals

Police and Fire

police
fire

General Purposes

law and procedure; parliamentary and court work
ceremonial, hospitality
registration of births, deaths and marriages
home defence
miscellaneous

8.11 We believe that this service committee structure would be suitable in Central and Fife, neither of which should require any other standing service committees. It is also applicable in Borders, Dumfries and Galloway, and Highland subject to provision being made for libraries, which in these regions could reside with either the education committee or the leisure and recreation committee. Regional responsibility for building control we deal with later at paragraph 8.16.

8.12 In Lothian, Grampian and Tayside we consider that additional committee provision will be required in the transportation and basic services field because of the likely scale of activities and also to oversee the management of the authorities' public transport undertakings. Three possibilities are:

△ three separate standing committees responsible respectively for roads, for sewerage and water services and for public transport

△ two separate standing sub-committees of the parent transportation and basic services committee, responsible for roads and for sewerage and water services respectively, and a separate standing committee for public transport

△ one parent committee, transportation and basic services, with three sub-committees.

On balance we prefer the last arrangement.

8.13 In Strathclyde we consider that there will be a requirement for:

△ a separate standing committee to assume the responsibilities of the Passenger Transport Authority

△ three standing committees for roads, sewerage and water or alternatively three standing sub-committees of the parent committee.

8.14 In those regions where joint arrangements have been prescribed for police and fire there will be separate statutory joint committees.

Resource committee structure

8.15 All regions will require standing committees or sub-committees with responsibility for:

△ finance

△ manpower

△ planning and development.

We have already stressed the cardinal importance of effective allocation of resources which is a key role of the policy and resources committee. We therefore re-emphasise the necessity for a strong element of linked membership between these committees and the policy and resources committee. Alternatively, as we indicated in Chapter 4, resource sub-committees of the policy and resources committee could be created.

8.16 The role of the planning and development committee has already been described in paragraph 6.43. This committee will have additional responsibilities in Highland, Borders, and Dumfries and Galloway, which are general planning authorities, and should also be responsible for building control, with a sub-committee arrangement as suggested in paragraph 6.67.

8.17 Because of the reduction in the number of councillors it seems inevitable that members will require to specialise to some extent in order to facilitate the effective despatch of business, and that the size of the service committees and the resource committees will require to be limited, consistent with the need for adequate representation. We therefore consider that no committee should consist of more than one third of the members of the full council. In Borders, however, with a council membership of only 23, this limit might have to be exceeded.

Other committees

8.18 In addition to the standing and statutory joint committees already mentioned, we have suggested, in Chapter 6, a requirement for liaison committees between a region and its districts. In all regions, except perhaps Strathclyde, we consider that such committees should be set up for each district. In Strathclyde which has 15 districts, this arrangement may be considered to place too heavy a demand on regional councillors, in which case a suitable grouping of districts would be required.

8.19 In the case of Strathclyde, also, we have earlier referred to the possible need for area committees of regional councillors with responsibility for the general oversight of devolved regional services. We feel that their areas should correspond with the boundaries eventually decided upon for the sub-regional management level of the main regional services.

8.20 The proposed committee arrangements for the various regions are shown in Diagrams 1 and 2.

Officer structure

8.21 In the basic officer structure we envisage the following separate departments:

△ education

△ social work

△ engineering and technical services

△ leisure and recreation

△ consumer protection

△ physical planning

△ architecture

75

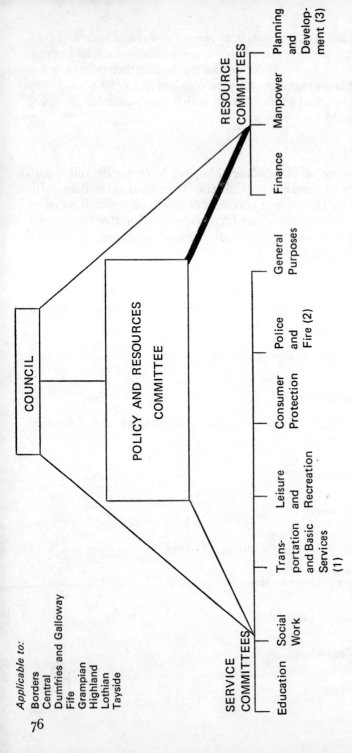

Applicable to:
Borders
Central
Dumfries and Galloway
Fife
Grampian
Highland
Lothian
Tayside

COUNCIL

POLICY AND RESOURCES COMMITTEE

RESOURCE COMMITTEES

Planning and Development (3)

Manpower

Finance

SERVICE COMMITTEES

Education

Social Work

Transportation and Basic Services (1)

Leisure and Recreation

Consumer Protection

Police and Fire (2)

General Purposes

[1] Except in Lothian, Grampian and Tayside which would have separate committees or sub-committees for roads, for sewerage and water and for public transport.

[2] Except in Highland, Borders and Lothian where there will be joint committees.

[3] Highland, Borders, and Dumfries and Galloway would also require sub-committees for planning and building applications.

Diagram 1 REGIONAL COMMITTEE STRUCTURE

Applicable to Strathclyde

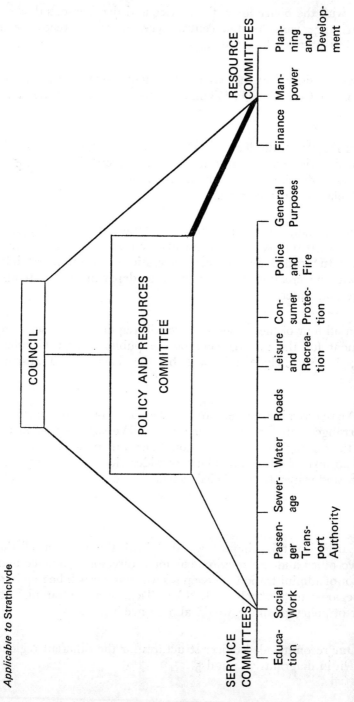

Diagram 2 REGIONAL COMMITTEE STRUCTURE

77

together with the police force, fire service and the assessor's department. Arrangements for the central services have already been discussed at paragraphs 8.5–8.8.

8.22 We consider that the basic departmental structure would be applicable in Central, Fife, Highland, Borders, and Dumfries and Galloway.

8.23 In Highland, Borders, and Dumfries and Galloway, responsibility for libraries may be given to leisure and recreation or perhaps to education. Building control should constitute a section within the physical planning department.

8.24 In Lothian, Tayside and Grampian there will probably be a need to have two separate departments for roads and for sewerage and water. In Strathclyde, the scale of operations will almost certainly necessitate the creation of three separate departments for roads, sewerage and water.

8.25 In all four of these regions there will require to be a separate department for the management of the public transport undertakings; in Strathclyde this will be the Passenger Transport Executive.

8.26 We referred in Chapter 6 to the need for sub-regional management arrangements for the major services. We suggest that in all regions the sub-regional structure should be set up on a district basis, subject to hydrological boundary considerations in the case of sewerage and water. In Strathclyde we have also suggested the likely requirement for an intermediate level of management for the major services.

8.27 Earlier in this chapter we described the concept of the executive office and the requirement for a director of finance and a director of administration. These posts we consider will be required in all regions; in Strathclyde, Lothian, Tayside and Grampian, a director of policy planning would also be needed.

8.28 Our recommended officer structures for the different regions are shown in diagrams 3, 4 and 5.

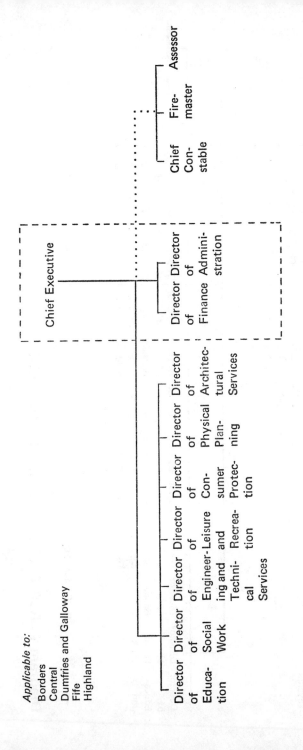

Applicable to:
Borders
Central
Dumfries and Galloway
Fife
Highland

Chief Executive

Director of Education

Director of Social Work

Director of Engineering and Technical Services

Director of Leisure and Recreation

Director of Consumer Protection

Director of Physical Planning

Director of Architectural Services

Director of Finance

Director of Administration

Chief Constable

Fire-master

Assessor

– – – – the Executive Office

Diagram 3 REGIONAL OFFICER STRUCTURE

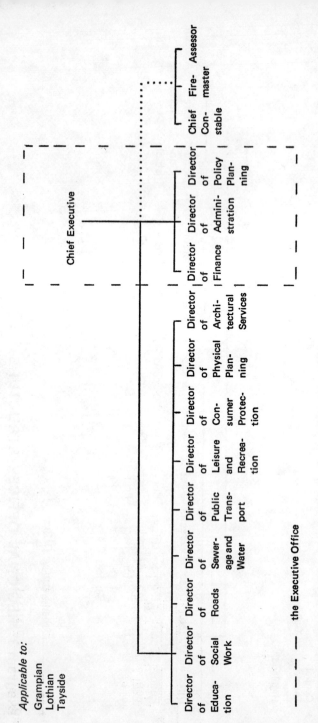

Applicable to:
Grampian
Lothian
Tayside

Chief Executive

Director of Education

Director of Social Work

Director of Roads

Director of Sewerage and Water

Director of Public Transport

Director of Leisure and Recreation

Director of Consumer Protection

Director of Physical Planning

Director of Architectural Services

Director of Finance

Director of Administration

Director of Policy Planning

Chief Constable

Fire-master

Assessor

— — — the Executive Office

Diagram 4 REGIONAL OFFICER STRUCTURE

Applicable to Strathclyde

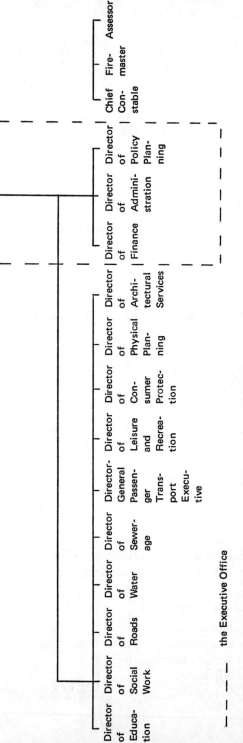

Diagram 5 REGIONAL OFFICER STRUCTURE

8.29 The basic organisational pattern illustrated on page 69 is also applicable to the districts as is the need for the corporate approach, although its detailed application will vary depending on the size of the district. In the smallest districts of all, with councils of less than 15 members, we could envisage the council itself performing the role of the policy and resources committee. Similarly the officer structure in these districts will be very limited in extent.

Service committee structure

8.30 We consider that all districts except the very smallest will require four service committees as follows:

Housing

assessment of need
design, construction and improvement
housing management

Environmental Health

sanitary services
cleansing
burial grounds and crematoria
markets and slaughterhouses

Leisure and Recreation

assessment of need
provision and management of recreational facilities, including parks, swimming baths, sports centres, community centres, halls and theatres
provision and management of libraries and museums (except districts in Highland, Borders, and Dumfries and Galloway)

General Purposes

regulation and licensing
law and procedure, parliamentary and court work
ceremonial, hospitality
miscellaneous.

Responsibility for planning applications and for building control is discussed in paragraph 8.36 below.

8.31 In the larger districts the volume and complexity of business will almost certainly demand the creation of standing sub-committees of all the committees except general purposes.

8.32 In the smallest districts within the three general planning regions it is possible that the functions of the environmental health and the leisure and recreation committees could be grouped together in one committee.

Resource committee structure

8.33 In the large urban districts, as in the regions, we consider that there will be the same requirement for three resource committees or sub-committees:

△ finance

△ manpower

△ planning and development

with the same strong links with the policy and resources committee as already described.

8.34 In the smaller districts we consider that the oversight of the main elements of resources could be the responsibility of the policy and resources committee itself and that separate resource committees or sub-committees would not be needed, subject to the requirement mentioned at paragraph 8.36 below.

8.35 The policy and resources committee must clearly be involved in the policy aspects of the local plan, mirroring the same responsibilities which its regional equivalent has in relation to the structure plan.

8.36 However, all districts, except those in the regions which are general planning authorities, will also be responsible for development control and building control. We believe that the volume of applications and the need to deal speedily with them will require additional committee arrangements. In the larger districts this could be achieved through two sub-committees of the planning and development committee, as suggested in paragraph 6.67. In the smaller districts a planning and development committee would also be required, again with the same sub-committee arrangement; this committee could also be concerned with the land-use aspects of local plan preparation.

8.37 Our observations on committee size at paragraph 8.17 are also applicable to districts although in many of the smaller districts it may be impracticable to keep committee membership to one-third of the full council.

Other committees

8.38 In Chapter 6 and in paragraph 8.18 we pointed out the need for liaison committee arrangements between the region and its districts. Detailed arrangements for membership of such committees will be made by the new authorities themselves; however we believe that the district policy and resources committee should be strongly represented.

8.39 The proposed committee arrangements for districts are shown in Diagrams 6 and 7.

Officer structure

8.40 We consider that all districts should appoint a chief executive. In the largest districts we believe that the executive office arrangement will also be necessary. In the smaller districts, the reduced scale and complexity of activities together with economic considerations would make it necessary and practicable that the chief executive should assume direct responsibility himself for a main department.

Large Districts

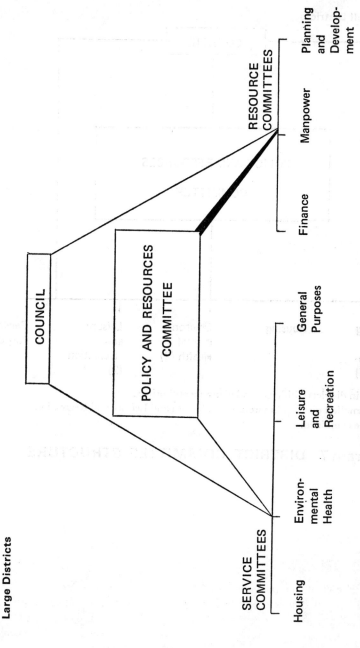

Diagram 6 DISTRICT COMMITTEE STRUCTURE

85

Small Districts

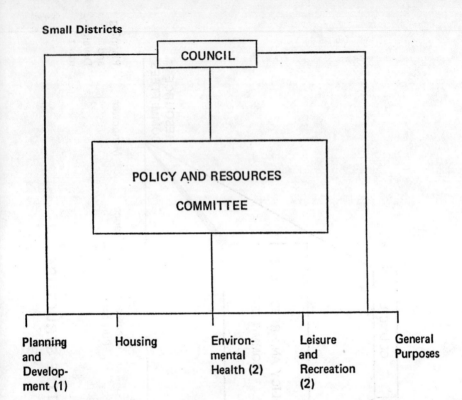

¹ Except in districts within general planning authorities.
² In the smallest districts Environmental Health and Leisure and Recreation
   could be combined.

Diagram 7   DISTRICT COMMITTEE STRUCTURE

8.41 Subject to possible groupings discussed below the basic officer structure would contain the following units:

△ housing

△ physical planning and building control (except in general planning authority areas)

△ cleansing

△ sanitary services

△ libraries (except in general planning authority areas)

△ museums

△ swimming pools and sports centres

△ parks and other recreational facilities

together with finance, legal and administration, and architectural services. The same basic need for the other central support services will exist in all districts but the degree and extent to which provision will be made will vary extensively—from comprehensive departments or sections in the largest districts down to the allocation of several of them to one individual officer. Some districts may also take over a general direct labour force from existing authorities.

8.42 The most important service in districts will be housing; we stress that the scope of this task assumes totally different, and increased, dimensions in certain areas by the addition of counties' landward housing stock to that of the existing burghs—in some cases doubling it.

8.43 We accept the need for a comprehensive housing management department under a director of housing in the larger districts. We would not envisage the director of housing being directly responsible for housing construction (although he must be involved in the preparation of the necessary briefs) or necessarily having direct control over maintenance personnel in those districts which have a sizeable building and works capability.

8.44 We have already indicated the possibility that some small districts may not be able to justify their own architectural service, in which case joint or agency arrangements or the use of outside architects would be required. Joint arrangements for libraries may also be desirable in the smaller districts.

8.45 There are several possible ways in which some of the units listed in paragraph 8.41 could be grouped depending on the size of district, scale and complexity of activities and the importance of particular services in the light of individual local needs. In Chapter 6 we discussed the main possibilities, which are:

△ a combination of some or all of the technical services such as architecture, building and works, and perhaps also physical planning

△ a grouping of cleansing and sanitary services

△ a leisure and recreation grouping comprising parks, swimming pools, sports centres and other facilities.

8.46 We have given careful consideration to these possibilities and show our proposed officer structures for large and small districts in diagrams 8 and 9.

8.47 We highlighted in Chapter 2 the very wide range in size of districts. While we show recommended structures for large and for small districts we consider it undesirable to attempt a rigid classification of the proposed authorities into one category or the other. Rather the proposed structures should be regarded as guide-lines which can be adapted in the light of particular local circumstances. In the case of the smallest districts of all; such as Skye and Lochalsh, it is likely that even the form of structure shown in diagram 9 may be too elaborate for local needs; an arrangement with, for example three chief officers responsible for legal and administration, finance and technical functions may suffice.

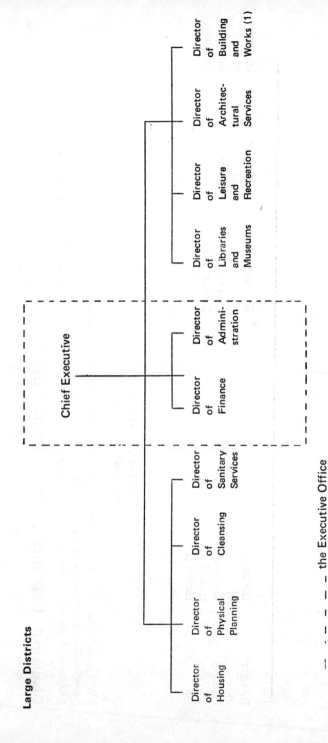

Large Districts

Chief Executive

Director of Housing

Director of Physical Planning

Director of Cleansing

Director of Sanitary Services

Director of Finance

Director of Administration

Director of Libraries and Museums

Director of Leisure and Recreation

Director of Architectural Services

Director of Building and Works (1)

– – – – – – the Executive Office

[1] Dependent on existence and scale of direct works departments.

Diagram 8 DISTRICT OFFICER STRUCTURE

Small Districts

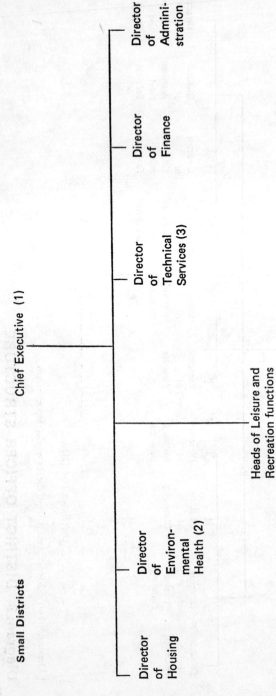

Chief Executive (1)

Director of Housing

Director of Environmental Health (2)

Heads of Leisure and Recreation functions

Director of Technical Services (3)

Director of Finance

Director of Administration

[1] Will probably have direct responsibility as a director of one of the main departments.

[2] Responsible for cleansing and sanitary services.

[3] Responsible for architecture, direct works and, where applicable, physical planning and building control.

Diagram 9 DISTRICT OFFICER STRUCTURE

ISLANDS

8.48 The islands, being most-purpose authorities, will not have the same co-ordination difficulties as the rest of Scotland. Indeed in Orkney and Shetland, apart from the disappearance of burghs and districts, there is little change in overall responsibility. In Western Isles on the other hand, the challenge is that of creating an effective organisation from the existing outposted elements of two counties.

8.49 The major problems which we anticipate in the islands are those caused by geography and by the relatively small resources which they will have at their disposal. The former accentuates the need for local devolution, subject to not spreading scarce staff resources too thinly. The latter would suggest that in addition to police and fire, there could well be a need for joint arrangements with neighbouring regions for the use of certain facilities or specialist staff which cannot economically be provided locally.

Committee structure

8.50 We recommend that each of the islands authorities should appoint a policy and resources committee. We do not consider that separate resource committees would be required. In Orkney and Shetland, however, the extensive demands which oil development will continue to make on development planning and control will almost certainly necessitate a separate committee.

8.51 In addition to the above, we consider that the following standing committees will be required in the islands authorities:

△ education

△ social work

△ transportation and basic services

△ leisure and recreation

△ housing

△ environmental health and control

△ general purposes.

The responsibilities of these committees would be as already specified in our recommendations for regions and districts except for the environmental health and control committee, which would embrace the remits suggested for the regional consumer protection and district environmental health committees. We are conscious of the demands which will be placed on the small number of members in the islands authorities and it is possible that they may consider some further grouping of committees (*eg* leisure and recreation with education) to be desirable. There is also the requirement for joint committees for police and fire.

8.52 In the absence of districts and because of the desirability of local devolution, we see the links with the new community councils being particularly important. The islands authorities may also consider it appropriate to delegate certain tasks to the community councils.

8.53 Our proposed committee structure for the islands authorities is illustrated in diagram 10.

Officer structure

8.54 We believe that there will be a requirement for the following departments:

△ education

△ social work

△ engineering and technical services

△ consumer protection and environmental health

△ housing

△ leisure and recreation

together with finance, and legal and administration.

8.55 We attach much importance to the proper development of leisure and recreational provisions and consider that a separate

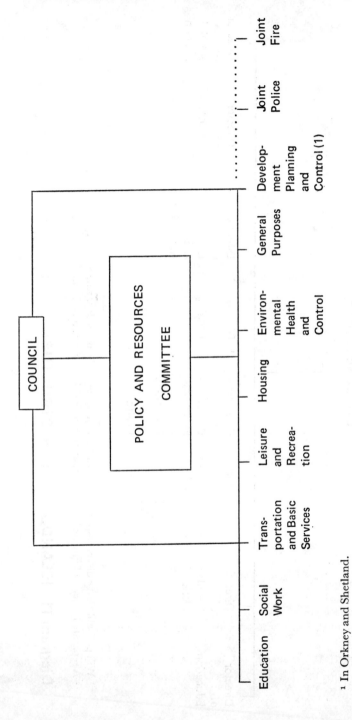

Diagram 10 ISLANDS COMMITTEE STRUCTURE

[1] In Orkney and Shetland.

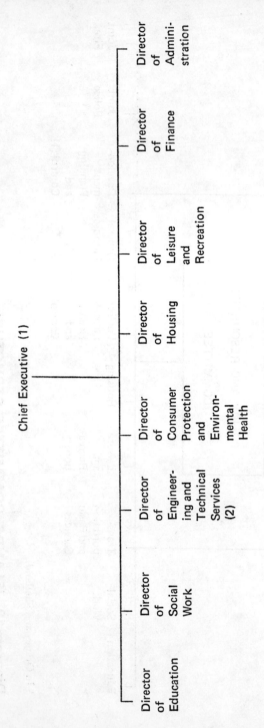

94

Chief Executive (1)

| Director of Education | Director of Social Work | Director of Engineering and Technical Services (2) | Director of Consumer Protection and Environmental Health | Director of Housing | Director of Leisure and Recreation | Director of Finance | Director of Administration |

[1] Will probably have direct responsibility as a director of one of the main departments.
[2] A separate Director of Physical Planning may be required in Orkney and Shetland.

Diagram 11 ISLANDS OFFICER STRUCTURE

department is justified, at least in the longer term. In the short term, however, practical considerations may suggest that this function should be located within the education department.

8.56 In Orkney and in Shetland, because of the importance of oil development as already mentioned, it is possible that physical planning may justify a separate department rather than be included within the engineering and technical services department as implied above.

8.57 Our recommended officer structure for the islands authorities is illustrated in diagram 11.

Chapter 9

Main points of the report

9.1 For reference purposes we consider it convenient to summarise the main points of the report. We stress, however, that these should not be read outwith the context of the full report.

Chapter 2—the basis of the proposed reform

9.2 The proposed reform produces authorities which vary substantially in population and geographical area (*paragraphs 2.2 to 2.4*).

9.3 No single pattern of organisation will fit all authorities, even authorities of the same type (*paragraph 2.6*).

9.4 Certain features of the reform impose constraints on the choice of possible structures for the new authorities (*paragraphs 2.8 to 2.12*).

Chapter 3—the current situation in Scotland

9.5 With certain exceptions, the existing organisations in Scotland are still largely based on the traditional pattern (*paragraph 3.1*).

9.6 In general, the process of policy formulation is carried out independently within each service committee and its associated department (*paragraph 3.5*).

9.7 The finance committee tries to exercise a co-ordinating role but its effectiveness is limited (*paragraph 3.6*).

9.8 Some authorities are aware of the limitations of the present set-up and a few have made significant organisational changes (*paragraphs 3.10 to 3.17*).

9.9   The strengths of the professional will still be needed in the new authorities (*paragraph 3.19*).

9.10   A new approach to management is, however, required in the new authorities (*paragraph 3.20*).

Chapter 4—cornerstones of the new structures

9.11   The need in principle for the corporate approach to the management of the new authorities is clearly established (*paragraphs 4.2 to 4.4*).

9.12   The ultimate power of decision must remain with the council which will require co-ordinated advice not only from officers but from an appropriate body of its own members (*paragraph 4.7*).

9.13   Both elected members and officers must be involved in varying degrees at every stage of the management process (*paragraph 4.8*).

9.14   The member's constituency role is vital and represents a fundamental communication link (*paragraph 4.11*).

9.15   Organisations based on the cabinet and management board systems would not permit adequate participation by all members and are therefore rejected (*paragraphs 4.13 to 4.16*).

9.16   In all but the smallest authorities there should be a policy and resources committee to provide co-ordinated policy advice to the council (*paragraph 4.18*).

9.17   The service committees should be responsible for policy formulation and implementation in their own spheres, within the council's overall policy, and should have direct access to the council (*paragraph 4.19*).

9.18   The larger authorities will require resource committees or sub-committees responsible for overall allocation and control of finance, manpower and land. There should be a substantial element of common membership between these committees and the policy and resources committee (*paragraph 4.20*).

9.19 Performance review should be a function of the policy and resources committee itself (*paragraph 4.21*).

9.20 The policy and resources committee must be able to command the support of the council and the other committees. It should therefore comprise the leading members of the council (*paragraph 4.23*).

9.21 Alternative compositions of the policy and resources committee are suggested (*paragraphs 4.25 to 4.28*).

9.22 Every authority should appoint a chief executive, with defined authority over the other chief officers, to lead the management team. The post of chief executive should be open to all officers irrespective of professional qualifications (*paragraphs 4.30 to 4.31*).

9.23 The chief executive should not have direct responsibility for a major department except in smaller authorities (*paragraph 4.32*).

9.24 Members of the officers' management team should be concerned with the overall objectives of the authority, not solely with the activities of their own departments (*paragraph 4.33*).

Chapter 5—the corporate management process

9.25 The corporate process represents a total style of management, not merely an isolated technique (*paragraph 5.1*).

9.26 The objective of corporate management is to achieve a unified approach to meeting the needs of the community (*paragraph 5.3*).

9.27 Corporate management properly applied should significantly increase the elected members' scope for effective decision-making and control (*paragraphs 5.4 to 5.6*).

9.28 The policy plan is the master from which all other plans derive and to which they contribute (*paragraph 5.9*).

9.29 Policy planning and structure and local planning are not the exclusive province of the physical planner; all disciplines within the authority must contribute (*paragraph 5.13*).

9.30 A gradualist approach to policy planning is advocated and the possible main stages are outlined (*paragraph 5.16*).

9.31 Committees and departments should be organised as far as practicable on a programme area basis. Where this would prove unwieldy in the case of departments, the programme area team approach should be adopted (*paragraphs 5.18 to 5.20*).

9.32 Policy planning units should be set up in the larger authorities which will also require a central research and intelligence capability (*paragraphs 5.22 to 5.23*).

9.33 Close and harmonious co-operation among the new authorities will be vital (*paragraph 5.24*).

Chapter 6—the service functions

9.34 Each of the service functions is examined to establish:

△   the main tasks performed

△   the links with other services

△   the links with the public and with outside organisations.

Organisational implications for each service are considered (*throughout*).

9.35 Possible arrangements for achieving the necessary co-operation and co-ordination between services and between authorities are suggested (*paragraph 6.15*).

9.36 There should be a 'one door' approach for the public to all local authority services (*paragraph 6.16*).

9.37 The local organisation will be a fundamental requirement in providing effective service. Extensive devolution of the major regional services will be necessary. Sub-regional boundaries should be the same for all services as far as possible and should be co-terminous with districts or groups of districts (*paragraph 6.75*).

9.38 The local management units should have defined areas of accountability and should be able to act without having to refer everything upwards (*paragraph 6.76*).

Chapter 7—the central support services

9.39 Each of the central support functions is examined, their main tasks reviewed, links with service departments considered and organisational implications identified (*throughout*).

9.40 The central support functions should be regarded as skills available to and under the direction of the chief executive and the management team. The reporting line in most cases should be through the executive office or to a nominated member of the management team (*paragraph 7.51 and throughout*).

9.41 There will be wide variation in the degree of development of the central support functions depending on the size and scope of authorities (*paragraph 7.52*).

Chapter 8—recommended structures for the new authorities

9.42 The immense demands which will be made on the chief executive in the larger authorities necessitate a formalised arrangement for his support. The concept of the 'executive office' is recommended. This should comprise the chief executive and directors of finance, administration and, in certain cases, policy planning (*paragraphs 8.4 to 8.8*).

9.43 Committee and officer structures applicable to the different types and sizes of authority are recommended (*paragraphs 8.10 to 8.57*).

Appendices

Appendix
Number

1   Conduct of the study

2   Authorities submitting information on present organisation

3   Professional organisations submitting evidence or otherwise assisting

4   Other organisations providing assistance

5   Joint advisory committees and existing authorities submitting views on consultation paper

6   The new authorities—selected statistics

7   The proposed allocation of functions

8   Illustration of range of population of the new authorities

9   City of Dundee—new officer structure

10   Terms of reference for the policy and resources committee

11   Terms of reference for the chief executive

12   The service functions—illustration of possible division of tasks between region and sub-region.

Appendix 1

Conduct of the study

1   The respective responsibilities of the Steering Committee of members, the Advisory Group of officials and the Central Advisory Unit are outlined in the Introduction. The general pattern of working, within an overall programme approved by the Steering Committee, was as follows:

△   the detailed investigations were carried out mainly by the Central Advisory Unit and in part by individual members of the Advisory Group

△   resulting from tnis, papers on major topics were prepared by the Central Advisory Unit for consideration in depth at joint working sessions of the Advisory Group and the Unit

△   the Steering Committee met regularly to review progress, to give guidance as required and to consider and approve the main conclusions from the study.

2   At the outset we wrote to all counties, cities and large and small burghs in Scotland to obtain the basic details of their present forms of organisation and to discover whether any significant changes had been made within recent years. A list of those authorities which supplied relevant information is given at Appendix 2. At later stages of the investigation we were able, in many cases, to probe behind the basic details in both formal and informal discussions with members and officers, thus gaining a deeper insight into the practical working of the different types of existing authority.

3   We established early contact with the various professional associations and staff organisations representing local government officers within Scotland. Each organisation was invited to submit

to the Director of the Central Advisory Unit their considered views on relevant organisational and management topics, and was also invited to have preliminary discussions with the Director. In the event, separate meetings took place with representatives of virtually all the professional bodies before their submissions were prepared, and in several cases further meetings were held to discuss and amplify draft or final submissions. A list of all organisations which provided evidence or otherwise assisted is shown at Appendix 3.

4   Liaison was also established and maintained with other organisations within local government, such as LAMSAC, with relevant central government departments, academic institutions and with the Scottish central offices of the main political parties. Many of these provided valuable assistance, often on an informal basis, and again their names are recorded at Appendix 4.

5   We kept in touch from an early stage with the investigations of the English Working Group on Management Structures (the Bains Committee), and also had the benefit of a joint working session with members of the Bains Committee.

6   At around the same time as our own Group was formed, joint advisory committees of elected members were set up in the areas of the proposed new Scottish authorities to initiate and control the work of preparing for reorganisation, with the assistance of working parties of officers. We made early contact with all of the joint advisory committees. Virtually all have subsequently been most helpful in keeping us fully informed of their activities and findings and, in several cases, inviting us to attend and participate in committee and working party meetings. For our part, we offered assistance to the committees and working parties, through our Central Advisory Unit, in the form of general advice on planning and co-ordinating their activities and in the provision of fact-finding questionnaires for use in the first major phase of changeover preparation. Our offer of help was accepted in thirty cases.

7   Our consultations with the joint advisory committees and visits made to authorities are described in paragraphs 1.9 to 1.12 of the report. Appendix 5 lists those committees and existing authorities which expressed views on our consultation paper and also indicates those which we visited.

Authorities submitting information on present organisation

COUNTIES

Aberdeen
Argyll
Ayr
Banff
Berwick
Caithness
Clackmannan
Dumfries
Dunbarton
East Lothian
Fife
Inverness
Kincardine
Kinross
Kirkcudbright
Lanark
Midlothian
Peebles
Perth
Ross & Cromarty
Roxburgh
Selkirk
Wigtown

CITIES

Aberdeen
Dundee
Edinburgh
Glasgow

LARGE BURGHS

Airdrie
Arbroath
Ayr
Clydebank
Coatbridge
Dumbarton
Dumfries
Dunfermline
East Kilbride
Falkirk
Greenock
Hamilton
Kilmarnock
Kirkcaldy
Motherwell & Wishaw
Paisley
Perth
Rutherglen
Stirling

SMALL BURGHS

Alloa
Alva
Annan
Ardrossan
Armadale
Auchtermuchty
Barrhead
Bathgate

Biggar	Kirriemuir
Blairgowrie & Rattray	Ladybank
Bonnyrigg & Lasswade	Lanark
Brechin	Langholm
Bridge of Allan	Laurencekirk
Buckhaven & Methil	Lerwick
Buckie	Linlithgow
Burntisland	Loanhead
Carnoustie	Lochgilphead
Cockenzie & Port Seton	Lockerbie
Cove & Kilcreggan	Macduff
Crieff	Milngavie
Cumbernauld	Moffat
Cupar	Monifieth
Dalbeattie	Montrose
Denny & Dunipace	Musselburgh
Dornoch	Newton Stewart
Dunbar	North Berwick
Dunoon	Oban
Duns	Oldmeldrum
East Linton	Penicuik
Elgin	Pitlochry
Elie & Earlsferry	Prestwick
Findochty	Renfrew
Forfar	Rothes
Galashiels	Rothesay
Girvan	St Andrews
Hawick	Saltcoats
Helensburgh	Selkirk
Huntly	Stonehaven
Innerleithen	Stornoway
Inveraray	Stromness
Inverbervie	Tayport
Invergordon	Tranent
Inverurie	Troon
Kilsyth	Turriff
Kirkcudbright	Whithorn
Kirkintilloch	Wigtown
Kirkwall	

Professional organisations submitting evidence or otherwise assisting

Association of Chief Police Officers (Scotland)

Association of County Treasurers in Scotland

Association of Directors of Education in Scotland

Association of Directors of Social Work

Association of Lands Valuation Assessors of Scotland

Association of Local Government Engineers and Surveyors

Association of Public Analysts of Scotland

Association of Public Lighting Engineers (Scottish Section)

Association of Public Passenger Transport Operators 'A' (Scotland and Northern Ireland) Area

Association of Registrars in Scotland

Association of Reporters to Children's Panels

Association of Water Board Engineers (Scotland)

British Association of Social Workers (Scottish Region)

Chief Fire Officers Association (Scottish Branch)

County Planning Officers' Society for Scotland

County Surveyors' Society (Scottish Branch)—*via* Scottish Engineering Group

District Council Clerks Association of Scotland

Educational Institute of Scotland

Head Teachers Association of Scotland

Institute of Baths Management

Institute of Housing Managers

Institute of Housing Managers (Scottish Branch)

Institute of Municipal Building Management (Scottish Region)

Institute of Municipal Treasurers and Accountants (Scottish Branch)

Institute of Park and Recreation Administration

Institute of Public Cleansing (Scottish Centre)

Institute of Purchasing and Supply

Institute of Trading Standards Administration (Scottish Branch)

Institute of Water Pollution Control (Scottish Branch)

Institution of Municipal Engineers (Scottish Branch)

Institution of Water Engineers (Scottish Section)

Royal Incorporation of Architects in Scotland

Royal Institution of Chartered Surveyors, Scottish Branch

Royal Sanitary Association of Scotland

Royal Town Planning Institute (Scottish Branch)

Scottish Association of Resort Publicity Officers

Scottish County, City and Burgh Architects' Joint Association

Scottish Engineering Group

Scottish Institute of Environmental Health

Scottish Library Association

Scottish Local Government Management Services Group

Scottish Principal Educational Psychologists

Society of Clerks and Treasurers of Water Boards in Scotland

Society of County Clerks in Scotland

Society of County Engineers in Scotland—*via* Scottish Engineering Group

Society of Town Clerks in Scotland

Other organisations providing assistance

Bradford County Borough Council
Catholic Education Commission
Communist Party Scottish Committee
Conservative and Unionist Party in Scotland
Coventry County Borough Council
Greater London Council
Institute of Local Government Studies—Birmingham University
Labour Party Scottish Council
Local Authority Management Services and Computer Committee
Local Government Operational Research Unit
Local Government Research Unit—Paisley College of Technology
Local Government Training Board
National Association of Local Government Officers
National Joint Councils for Local Authorities' Services (Scottish Councils)
Planning Exchange, Glasgow
Regional Development Division, Scottish Office
Royal Institute of Public Administration
Scottish Churches' Council
Scottish Council of Social Service
Scottish Development Department
Scottish Education Department
Scottish Home and Health Department
Scottish Liberal Party
Scottish Local Authorities Special Housing Group
Scottish National Party

Scottish Sports Council

Social Work Services Group

Teesside County Borough Council

University of Edinburgh—Department of Social Administration

University of Strathclyde—Department of Politics

Working Group on Local Authority Management Structures
(the Bains Committee)

Joint advisory committees and existing authorities submitting views on consultation paper

Regional Joint Advisory Committees
*Borders
Dumfries and Galloway
Grampian
Lothian
Strathclyde

District Joint Advisory Committees
Annandale and Eskdale
Argyll
Badenoch and Strathspey
Caithness
Clackmannan
East Kilbride
*East Lothian
Gordon
Inverness
Kincardine and Deeside
Merrick
*Midlothian
Moray
Nithsdale
*Renfrew
Ross and Cromarty
Stewartry
Strathkelvin
Sutherland
*West Lothian

Existing Authorities
*Aberdeen Corporation
Airdrie Town Council

*Ayr County Council
Ayr Town Council
Banchory Town Council
Banff County Council
Bishopbriggs Town Council
*Cumbernauld Town Council
Dumbarton Town Council
*Dumfries County Council
Dunbarton County Council
*Dundee Corporation
Dunoon Town Council
*East Kilbride Town Council
*Edinburgh Corporation
*Fife County Council
*Glasgow Corporation
Greenock Town Council
Hamilton Town Council
*Hawick Town Council
*Inverness County Council
Kilmarnock Town Council
*Kirkcaldy Town Council
Kirkintilloch Town Council
*Lanarkshire County Council
Motherwell and Wishaw Town Council
*Perth County Council
Stirling County Council
*Stirling Town Council
Western No. 3 District Council Stirlingshire

* Visits made by Advisory Group and/or Director of Central Advisory Unit

Appendix 6

The new authorities— selected statistics

Region	District	1 Population ('000)	2 Electorate ('000)	Area (sq. miles)	Population Density (persons/ sq. mile)	3 Membership of Council	3 Membership on Regional Council
	Caithness	30	21	1217	24	16	8
	Sutherland	12	9	1737	7	12	4
	Ross & Cromarty	35	26	1930	18	20	10
	Skye & Lochalsh	10	7	958	10	10	3
	Lochaber	19	13	1724	11	12	5
	Inverness	49	35	1081	46	24	12
	Badenoch & Strathspey	9	7	1003	9	10	3
	Nairn	11	6	163	68	10	2
HIGHLAND	8	175	124	9813	18		47
	Moray	76	52	754	101	18	9
	Banff & Buchan	74	53	588	125	18	9
	Gordon	45	34	856	53	12	6
	Aberdeen City	208	156	71	2935	48	24
	Kincardine & Deeside	33	25	984	34	12	5
GRAMPIAN	5	437	320	3253	134		53
	Angus	84	61	785	108	22	10
	Dundee City	198	138	90	2195	44	22
	Perth & Kinross	115	80	2022	57	29	14
TAYSIDE	3	397	279	2897	137		46
	North East Fife	61	45	291	210	18	9
	Kirkcaldy	145	104	97	1496	36	18
	Dunfermline	121	84	117	1034	30	15
FIFE	3	328	233	505	650		42

Region	District	1 Population ('000)	2 Electorate ('000)	Area (sq. miles)	Population Density (persons/ sq. mile)	3 Membership of Council	3 Membership on Regional Council
	West Lothian	112	78	160	702	21	7
	Edinburgh City	472	353	105	4496	64	32
	Midlothian	80	55	138	581	15	5
	East Lothian	78	57	275	282	17	5
LOTHIAN	4	742	543	678	1094		49
	Tweeddale	14	10	347	39	10	3
	Ettrick Forest	32	24	525	62	16	8
	Roxburgh	36	27	544	66	16	8
	Merse	17	13	338	51	12	4
BORDERS	4	99	75	1754	56		23
	Clackmannan	46	32	63	731	12	6
	Stirling	76	55	839	91	20	10
	Falkirk	141	99	111	1271	36	18
CENTRAL	3	263	186	1013	260		34
	Argyll	65	46	2609	25	25	5
	Dunbarton	78	53	185	424	15	3
	Glasgow City	1147	778	148	7753	84	42
	Strathkelvin	102	69	100	1017	20	4
	Monklands	110	73	59	1862	20	4
	Motherwell	162	111	69	2378	30	6
	Cadzow	105	74	51	2052	20	4
	East Kilbride	78	54	130	603	16	3
	Lanark	53	38	512	104	14	3
	Renfrew	204	142	119	1710	40	8
	Inverclyde	109	75	61	1787	23	5
	Cunninghame	121	89	167	724	24	5
	Kilmarnock & Loudoun	81	60	145	559	16	3
	Kyle & Carrick	108	79	488	220	24	5
	Cumnock & Doon Valley	52	35	333	155	10	2
STRATHCLYDE	15	2578	1777	5176	498		102

Region	District	1 Population ('000)	2 Electorate ('000)	Area (sq. miles)	Population Density (persons/ sq. mile)	3 Membership of Council	3 Membership on Regional Council
	Merrick	30	21	662	45	14	7
	Stewartry	22	16	645	35	12	6
	Nithsdale	56	39	553	102	28	14
	Annandale & Eskdale	35	25	600	58	16	8
							—
DUMFRIES AND GALLOWAY	4	143	102	2460	58		35
Islands Authorities							
ORKNEY		17	13	376	46	23	
SHETLAND		18	13	552	32	22	
WESTERN ISLES		31	23	1119	27	30	

[1] Figures based on 1971 Census and rounded to nearest thousand.

[2] Figures based on 1973 Register of Electors and rounded to nearest thousand.

[3] Council membership figures are those proposed as at 30th June 1973, and may be subject, in some cases, to amendment before the Bill receives Royal Assent.

The proposed allocation of functions

Regional Authority Functions

Major planning and related services:

strategic planning; industrial development; transportation; roads, traffic management and road safety, passenger transport, ferry services, airports; water, sewerage, flood prevention and arterial drainage; countryside and tourism

Education
Social work
Regional housing
Police
Fire
Coast protection
Consumer protection
Weights and measures
Food standards and labelling
Diseases of animals
Community centres, parks and recreation[1]
Museums and art galleries[1]
Registration of births, deaths and marriages
Registration of electors

District Authority Functions

Local planning and associated services[2]—
urban development; countryside

Building control[2]
Housing
Community centres, parks and recreation[1]
Museums and art galleries[1]
Libraries[2]

Environmental health, including:

cleansing; refuse collection and disposal; food hygiene; Shops Act, etc.; clean air; markets and slaughterhouses; burial and cremation

Regulation and licensing, including:

cinemas and theatres; betting and gaming; taxis; house-to-house collections

Islands Authority Functions

The islands authorities will exercise all of the above functions subject to joint arrangements in the case of police and fire.

[1] Exercised concurrently by regional and district authorities

[2] Except in Highland, Dumfries and Galloway and Borders regions, where the function concerned will be regional

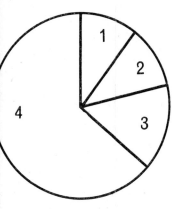

LOTHIAN

1 East Lothian
2 Midlothian
3 West Lothian
4 Edinburgh City

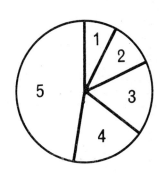

GRAMPIAN

1 Kincardine and
  Deeside
2 Gordon
3 Banff and Buchan
4 Moray
5 Aberdeen City

TAYS

1 Angu
2 Perth
3 Dund

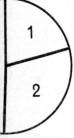

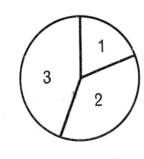

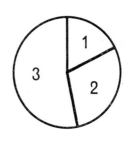

-IDE	**FIFE**	**CENTRAL**	
	1 North East Fife	1 Clackmannan	1
s	2 Dunfermline	2 Stirling	2
and Kinross	3 Kirkcaldy	3 Falkirk and	
ee City		Grangemouth	3
			4
			5
			6
			7
			8

Terms of reference for the policy and resources committee

1 To guide the council in the formulation of its policy objectives and priorities, and for this purpose to recommend to the council such forward programmes and other steps as may be necessary to achieve those objectives, either in whole or in part, during specific time spans. For this purpose to consider the broad social and economic needs of the authority and matters of comprehensive importance to the area, including the contents of structure and local plans. To advise the council generally as to its financial and economic policies.

2 Without prejudice to the duties and responsibilities of the service committees, to review the effectiveness of all the council's work and the standards and levels of service provided. To identify the need for new services and to keep under review the necessity for existing ones.

3 To submit to the council concurrent reports with the service committees upon new policies or changes in policy formulated by such committees, particularly those which may have significant impact upon the policy plan or the resources of the council.

4 To advise the council on the allocation and control of its financial, manpower and land resources.

5 To ensure that the organisation and management processes of the council are designed to make the most effective contribution to the achievement of the council's objectives. To keep them under review in the light of changing circumstances, making recommendations as necessary for change in either the committee or departmental structure, or the distribution of functions and responsibilities.

6 To be concerned, together with the appropriate other committees, in the appointment of heads of departments and any deputies.

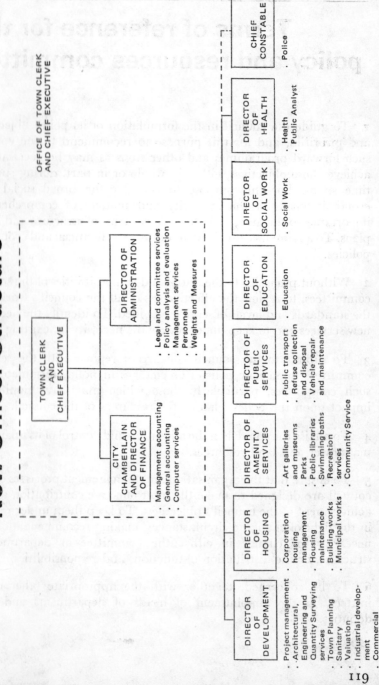

City of Dundee
New Officer Structure

OFFICE OF TOWN CLERK AND CHIEF EXECUTIVE

TOWN CLERK AND CHIEF EXECUTIVE

CITY CHAMBERLAIN AND DIRECTOR OF FINANCE
- Management accounting
- General accounting
- Computer services

DIRECTOR OF ADMINISTRATION
- Legal and committee services
- Policy analysis and evaluation
- Management services
- Personnel
- Weights and Measures

DIRECTOR OF DEVELOPMENT
- Project management
- Architectural, Engineering and Quantity Surveying services
- Town Planning
- Sanitary
- Valuation
- Industrial development
- Commercial properties

DIRECTOR OF HOUSING
- Corporation housing management
- Housing maintenance
- Building works
- Municipal works

DIRECTOR OF AMENITY SERVICES
- Art galleries and museums
- Parks
- Public libraries
- Swimming baths
- Recreation services
- Community Service

DIRECTOR OF PUBLIC SERVICES
- Public transport
- Refuse collection and disposal
- Vehicle repair and maintenance

DIRECTOR OF EDUCATION
- Education

DIRECTOR OF SOCIAL WORK
- Social Work

DIRECTOR OF HEALTH
- Health
- Public Analyst

CHIEF CONSTABLE
- Police

Illustration of range of population of the new authorities

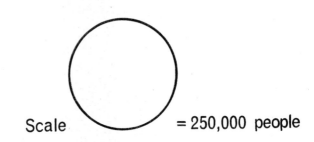

Scale = 250,000 people

 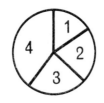

HIGHLAND	DUMFRIES AND GALLOWAY	BORDERS	WESTERN ISLES	SHETLAND	ORKNEY

HIGHLAND	DUMFRIES AND GALLOWAY	BORDERS
Skye and Lochalsh	1 Stewartry	1 Tweeddale
Badenoch and Strathspey	2 Merrick	2 Merse
Nairn	3 Annandale and Eskdale	3 Ettrick Forest
Sutherland	4 Nithsdale	4 Roxburgh
Lochaber		
Caithness		
Ross and Cromarty		
Inverness		

Terms of reference for the chief executive

1   The chief executive is the head of the council's paid service and shall have authority over all other officers so far as this is necessary for the efficient management and execution of the council's functions, except where:

  △   principal officers are exercising responsibilities imposed on them by statute

  △   the professional discretion or judgement of the principal officers is involved.

2   He is the leader of the officers' management team and, through the policy and resources committee, the council's principal adviser on matters of general policy. As such it is his responsibility to secure co-ordination of advice on the forward planning of objectives and services and to lead the management team in securing a corporate approach to the affairs of the authority generally.

3   Through his leadership of the officers' management team he is responsible for the efficient and effective implementation of the council's programmes and policies and for securing that the resources of the authority are most effectively deployed towards those ends.

4   Similarly, he shall keep under review the organisation and administration of the authority and shall make recommendations to the council through the policy and resources committee if he considers that major changes are required in the interests of effective management.

5   As head of the paid service it is his responsibility to ensure that effective and equitable manpower policies are developed and implemented throughout all departments of the authority in the interests both of the authority and the staff.

6   He is responsible for the maintenance of good internal and external relations.

The service functions

Illustration of Possible Division of Tasks between Region and Sub-Region

For each of the regional services we show those tasks which we think could be undertaken at a headquarters unit and those which might be carried out at a sub-regional level. We emphasise that the list of tasks shown under each service is by no means exhaustive and that their allocation between management levels is intended to be indicative only of what might be appropriate. Local circumstances will determine the precise allocation of tasks.

1 Education

Headquarters

△ formulating education policy

△ planning, providing and controlling the education services and developing the education programme

△ laying down organisational and operational guide-lines for pre-school, primary, secondary, further and special education, outdoor pursuits, youth employment, school meals

△ deployment of teaching and other staff

△ undertaking departmental personnel work, including training

△ laying down organisational and operational guide-lines for administrative services

△ providing specialist and advisory educational support services, including research and statistics.

Sub-Region

All tasks would be carried out within the framework of regional policy and procedures:

△ local administration of functions such as special education, youth employment, extra curricular activities, school meals, free meals and milk, school health, allocation and transfer of pupils, transport, attendance

△ administrative matters concerned with schools, colleges, youth centres, and play centres

△ operation of administrative systems and procedures connected with for, example, accounting, payment of wages and salaries, and supplies

△ personnel matters arising in respect of teaching and other staff

△ local arrangements in respect of deployment of staff

△ dealing with enquiries from members of the public (if not satisfactorily dealt with at school level).

2 Social work

Headquarters

△ formulating social work policy

△ planning, providing and controlling the social work services in respect of the needs of the homeless, the elderly, children and the disabled

△ developing the social work programme

△ laying down organisational and operational guide-lines for field services, case work, meals-on-wheels, fostering and adoption, day nurseries, the home help service and emergency service

△ in certain circumstances, placement in and management of establishments such as emergency housing, old people's homes, sheltered housing, children's homes, sheltered workshops, occupational centres, work centres, day centres and hostels

△ deployment of professional and other staff

△ undertaking departmental personnel work, including training

△ laying down organisational and operational guide-lines for administrative services

△ providing specialist and advisory social work services, including research and statistics

△ fostering links with voluntary organisations.

Sub-Region

All tasks would be carried out within the framework of regional policy and procedures:

△ local organisation, administration and supervision of social work field services and family case work, including referrals and assessments in respect of old people, the disabled, children being fostered or adopted and those under probation

△ liaison with the reporter to the children's panels and the preparation of reports

△ local organisation and administration of the home help service and the emergency services

△ in certain circumstances, placement in and management of establishments such as old people's homes, sheltered housing and children's homes

△ operation of administrative systems and procedures connected with, for example, accounting, payment of wages and salaries and supplies

△ personnel matters arising in respect of professional and administrative staffs

△ dealing with enquiries from members of the public

△ maintaining close working arrangements with voluntary organisations.

3 Roads and sewerage

Headquarters

△ formulating policy and preparing forward plans for a roads and sewerage and associated works programmes

△ planning and controlling the annual roads, lighting and sewerage programmes (in association with sub-region)

△ designing roads, bridges, lighting, sewerage and drainage schemes and sewage treatment plants and undertaking the associated tasks such as preparation of bills and checking tenders

△ setting up and controlling special project teams

△ laying down technical standards and procedures

△ laying down organisational and operational guide-lines for administrative services

△ deployment of professional and other staff

△ undertaking departmental personnel work, including training

△ dealing with technical enquiries

△ providing specialist and advisory engineering services such as traffic management, sewage treatment, research and statistics.

Sub-Region

All tasks would be carried out within the framework of regional policy and procedure:

△ planning and controlling the annual roads, lighting and sewerage programmes (in association with headquarters)

△ designing minor road works, footpaths, lighting schemes, sewerage and drainage works

△ organisation and management of a roads direct labour unit

△ organisation and management of lighting staff (electricians, drivers, labourers), plant and vehicles

△ organisation and management of a sewerage direct labour unit including operation of treatment plants

△ inspection and administration connected with street openings

△ undertaking inspection of sewers, drains and natural water courses and trade effluent control

△ undertaking operations connected with traffic management and control, including parking and accident prevention

△ dealing with roads and drainage emergencies

△ dealing with members of the public and with technical enquiries

△ operation of administrative systems and procedures connected with, for example, accounting, payment of wages and salaries and supplies

△ personnel matters arising in respect of engineering, technical and administrative staff.

4 Water

Headquarters

△ formulating policy and preparing forward plans in respect of catchment areas, supply and distribution requirements to meet the demand for water

△ planning and controlling the annual works programme in respect of building and engineering works

△ design work connected with buildings, reservoirs, pipelines and other installations

△ dealing with technical enquiries

△ deployment of engineering and other staff

△ undertaking departmental personnel work, including training

△ organisation of administrative services

△ planning emergency supply arrangements

Sub-Region

Tasks are operational and supervisory in nature:

△ laying and maintaining pipelines, installing supply points

△ operation and maintenance of water installations such as reservoirs, filtration and treatment plants

△ dealing with members of the public

△ dealing with emergencies.

5 Consumer protection

Headquarters

△ Assessing consumer protection needs in the area and providing the necessary staff, buildings and equipment

△ deployment of inspectors and clerical staff

△ maintenance of standards

△ utilisation and maintenance of test equipment and laboratory facilities

△ undertaking departmental personnel work, including training

△ organisation of administrative services

△ procedures associated with prosecution.

Sub-Region

△ inspection, testing and preparation of reports in respect of enforcement of statutes

△ maintenance of technical and administrative records

△ dealing with technical enquiries from local traders

△ dealing with enquiries and complaints from the public.

Printed in Scotland for Her Majesty's Stationery Office by D. J. Clark Limited, Glasgow
O.N. 525498 Dd. 955086 Gp. 53 K80 9/73

Her Majesty's Stationery Office

Government Bookshops

13a Castle Street, Edinburgh EH2 3AR
49 High Holborn, London WC1V 6HB
109 St Mary Street, Cardiff CF1 1JW
Brazennose Street, Manchester M60 8AS
50 Fairfax Street, Bristol BS1 3DE
258 Broad Street, Birmingham B1 2HE
80 Chichester Street, Belfast BT1 4JY

Government publications are also available through booksellers